BROWSERS
TO BUYERS

Proven Strategies for
Selling New Homes Online

· 2nd EDITION

BROWSERS to BUYERS

ACKNOWLEDGEMENTS

Inspiration comes from many places. I would like to use this opportunity to express my gratitude to those who have contributed to my life.

To the one person who has been with me through it all and supported me every step of the way; without my beautiful wife, I would be nothing. I love you, Cori.

To my two boys, Scott and Nate—the coolest kids I know.

To Myers Barnes, the catalyst and idea man—thank you for your encouragement and help. You have changed my life.

To Greg Simmons, for giving me a chance and the opportunity to succeed.

To my mother and father, who taught me the lessons of life and gave me the tools I need to make it in this world.

And to God, from whom all blessings flow.

FOREWORD

The ancient proverb instructs, "When the student is ready, the teacher will appear."

My relationship with Mike began when he was my student and I was counseling him on how to establish an internet sales department for my good friend and favorite homebuilder.

Within days, Mike's brilliance became evident and I was no longer counseling, but collaborating with him. Shortly thereafter, I reinterpreted the proverb to read, "When the teacher is ready, the student will appear." The roles were reversed and I was learning from Mike.

Now, it's your turn. Thanks to this marvelous manual, you will discover how to attract and track online new home buyers. Whether you are on the information highway or a digital dirt road, Mike simplifies the complex process and tells you step by step how to establish the evolving role of an Online Sales Counselor. Follow his instruction and you will learn how to close more online leads—automatically, confidently, and professionally—and make a favorable impression with every home buyer who visits your website.

Mike is, without question, the master of the internet. He delivers his message as someone who knows what he's talking about because he has learned from experience. What he teaches not only makes sense, but is also simple to follow and easy to implement. He is literally the heavyweight champion of the world for online, real estate sales.

So, if you're ready to be a student, the teacher has arrived.

Good selling,

Myers Barnes
President, Myers Barnes Associates

INTRODUCTION

Come gather 'round, people,
Wherever you roam,
And admit that the waters
Around you have grown,
And accept it that soon
You'll be drenched to the bone.
If your time to you
Is worth savin'
Then you better start swimmin'
Or you'll sink like a stone
For the times, they are a-changin'.

Come writers and critics
Who prophesize with your pen,
And keep your eyes wide,
The chance won't come again,
And don't speak too soon
For the wheel's still in spin,
And there's no tellin' who
That it's namin'.
For the loser now
Will be later to win
For the times, they are a-changin'.

- Bob Dylan

The times, they are a-changin'. This has never been more true than today. I have a running joke—that the worst thing I ever did was write a book about the internet. What was I thinking? By the time the manuscript goes to the printer, something has changed. And I'm thinking, "If I'd only waited a bit longer." But it wouldn't matter. The internet changes at the speed of light. Everything is shifting—shopping, dining, entertainment, communication, and yes, home buying.

As I write this, six years have passed since this book was originally published. Think about the changes that have occurred in both the online world and the home building industry. Mobile apps and marketing weren't commonplace then. Zillow and Trulia were in start-up mode; Facebook was just a bright, shiny object; and my precious iPhone was just a glimmer in Steve Jobs' eye.

And six years ago, the housing bubble had not yet burst.

Many talking heads blame the housing industry for the greatest financial crisis since the great depression. Fault or no fault, we took a beating. Home prices were off by 20, 30, 50 percent from the peaks, and building levels have sunk to all-time lows since 2008. Saying it has been tough is an understatement.

We have established a new normal. In this culture, the ones who have managed to survive the pummeling onslaught are just that—survivors. They are leaner, meaner, stronger, and smarter.

But the worst is behind us now. We are on the way out! It's time to reclaim your position and make your mark in the homebuilding industry, but you are running out of time. The competition grows more sophisticated every day, which puts your market share at risk. Why? Because the internet has leveled the playing field. No longer does traditional marketing and advertising rule the world of homebuilders. They have discovered the broad-reaching power of marketing on the Web. Hopefully, you have recognized this as well and are ready to jump-start your Online Sales Program.

Welcome to the New World

Now let's talk about the online world. Holy cow! Massive changes have taken place over the past six years. When this book was first published, I didn't include even one mention of social networking, blogging, Facebook, or Twitter. Smartphones had not yet achieved their current IQ. Google was just buying a start-up called YouTube. The Kindle was one year away from being released by Amazon.

What blows my mind is how many people and companies out there have severe cases of SHS (Same Haircut Syndrome). You know what I'm talking about—20 years ago, your Aunt Cheryl got the Farrah Fawcett hairstyle and still tries to rock it. She won't change the style—she doesn't WANT to change it. It's comfortable and she still thinks she looks good. This is how I refer to the people who choose to ignore the obvious—that technology can revolutionize your business. But you have to accept it first.

This new selling climate requires us to be better, stronger, faster, and more efficient. The online tools at our disposal (most of which are free or low cost) can do that. We just need to have the desire to learn and change the way we have always done things. Don't get stuck with that same haircut! Seriously. Take a look in the mirror, because you might need to change things up.

If you still need convincing, here are five reasons you need an Online Sales Program:

1. Without one, you are losing sales to your competition.
2. An Online Sales Program is affordable to implement.
3. You are losing sales by not responding immediately to prospects.
4. You are losing customers by not responding frequently enough.
5. Your salespeople are handling internet leads incorrectly; many times, secret shops have shown there is no follow-up. To me, this is like stealing.

You would think the current challenges and opportunities in the homebuilding industry would motivate sales executives to adopt a "no lead left behind" mantra, making sure everyone fully worked every prospect. However, surveys have shown us that the opposite is true. In fact, almost half of the time, there are no responses to leads submitted from a website—this includes e-mails and calls. Excuse me? None? I can't even imagine that a business would give up so many potential sales! But it happens—and far too often!

In all of my findings, I only see about five percent of builders actually following up with leads correctly.

Think I'm pulling your leg? Just secret shop your agents. Fill out the form on your website, add full contact information, and wait 30 days. Spend a Friday or Saturday afternoon and call all of the sales agents. See how many agents will actually pick up the phone.

I'm not knocking your sales executives. I'm just saying the current system is broken. If most of our buyers are doing their research online and trying to contact us via e-mail and phone, shouldn't you have a system in place to manage those prospects? I've written—and now re-written—this guidebook to give you the formula to increase your overall home sales this year and for years to come. It will also ensure that you retain your current market share. When you apply this method, you will accelerate the buying process and drive those customers to your models who will ultimately purchase a home one out of three times.

And guess what? You don't have to be a technological wizard to grab your share of online new home sales. All you need is the formula and the process and you can create the same program that the top builders use.

From the Trenches

I wish this manual had been around when I was hired by a homebuilder in 2005 to implement an Online Sales Program. He was a forward-thinking builder who was taking a proactive step by realizing that he needed to expand his reach online. We were the first in our market to create a program and hire a dedicated person to handle the leads coming from our website. As a result of being the first to tackle the challenge, it took me time to research and create the program and implement a process to follow up with our internet leads.

Make no mistake. I thought I was hot stuff. I had been working in the online space since the late 90's and thought I possessed enough knowledge to pull together a program with ease. I had helped multiple businesses successfully move their presence and advertising online and I thought this experience would make a quick transition to the homebuilding space. What I underestimated were the intricacies involved in the buying process for a home. We aren't selling widgets here. This is the most expensive item many people will ever buy and an extremely complex sale. The rules changed and I was a little out of my comfort zone while I honed in on exactly what worked.

This manual is the result of thousands of e-mails and phone calls with prospects. The process I used was consistent with almost every customer. By utilizing a process, I was able to work with more customers and increase my conversion rates.

In addition to my responsibilities as the Online Sales Counselor, I also handled all of the website marketing, advertising, and promotion. Since my background is in web development, sales, and marketing, I naturally saw a tremendous opportunity in the homebuilding industry to successfully integrate online marketing. Many builders were hanging on for dear life to the old style of marketing and not realizing the power of marketing online. I wanted to pull them back from the edge and give them the tools to reshape their businesses.

I now provide consulting, coaching and sales training to builders all over the world. I have had the great opportunity to work with many of the industry leaders and teams of Online Sales Counselors. From this experience, I have seen the patterns and trends emerge from following hundreds of websites, seeing millions of dollars invested in online advertising, and watching thousands of leads flow through CRM systems every month. After a while, this activity starts to look like that scene from "The Matrix", where the patterns start to pop out from those green characters raining down the computer monitor. We know what works, we know what doesn't, and I plan to share that with you here.

This manual is a great tool for Sales Managers, Marketing Directors, and Online Sales Counselors—no matter where you are in the process. Whether you are just starting out or already have a program set up, the information in this second edition of Browsers to Buyers will help to build and strengthen your Online Sales Program.

The bottom line is that, if you follow these practices, you will increase your sales and ensure that you are not losing customers to your competition.

Chapter One

HOMEBUYERS
SHOP ONLINE

Why you need to pay attention to your online customers

Homebuilders have several different marketing avenues from which to choose. Most builders allocate a large portion of their marketing budget to traditional forms, such as print advertising, radio, and television commercials. Many builders have a website, but use it almost like an online brochure with fairly static information and low interactivity. Even those builders who have created a new website usually don't apply enough importance to the first impression that they are making on their customers. By harnessing the power of technology and the internet, a builder can level the playing field and start attracting customers through the company's website. The Information Age has changed how customers think and act and puts them in the driver's seat. Many builders have not taken the time to understand how to apply online marketing to their business model, which undervalues a large sector of home buyers.

Permission vs. Interruption

Most traditional forms of advertising and marketing that builders use are based on interruption. Magazine and newspaper ads, billboards, television and radio commercials all require consumers to stop what they are doing and pay attention to your message, whether they want to or not. This is how most marketing has been done for ages and where most builders allocate their time and marketing dollars. While some traditional forms of interruption marketing are still necessary—and yes, effective—builders are missing a large opportunity to affordably and consistently engage qualified customers.

This is where permission marketing comes into play. Permission marketing requests the permission of your customers to send them information and communicate with them on an ongoing basis. Every day, hundreds of thousands of potential customers are starting their searches online for new homes. By creating an interactive and engaging website and encouraging user interaction, you can capture these "leads" and start the permission marketing process. A website is the most effective way to gain a customer's permission when you ask them to provide their email address and contact information.

Once they grant that permission to communicate with them by providing your site with their contact information, you can qualify this customer and send targeted and affordable messages more frequently. With that frequency, customers will become familiar with you as a builder and your communication will garner their trust. Inevitably, trust will transform a browser into a buyer.

Why the internet?

During the past 15 years, technology has made its way into every aspect of our lives. With the mass production of the PC, mobile devices, and tablets, coupled with the integration of internet connectivity and web access, individuals and businesses have found new and exciting ways to capitalize on the increase of information that is readily available at our fingertips. Through the adoption of these new technologies and the widespread use of the internet, we have seen new, everyday activities evolve right before our eyes.

Instead of CDs, you can download songs over the internet to your mp3 player. Customers are ditching cable for sites like Hulu and Netflix streaming services. Bookstores have shut their doors, giving way to e-readers like Kindle and Nook, along with the proliferation of downloadable ebooks. Online news portals and blogs have replaced the daily reading of the newspaper. Shopping websites have almost eliminated paper catalogs. E-mail and texting have become the preferred methods of communication. Skype has trumped the long distance phone call and now most online users spend a good part of their time on Facebook catching up with friends, posting pictures, or whatever the latest game craze happens to be. Many Americans could not even imagine a day without internet connectivity.

What a difference 15 years can make. The overall number of connected Americans is quickly approaching 100 percent. One of the biggest changes ushered in by the internet is the method now used by businesses to connect with their customers. Some of the most successful companies in America were created to capitalize from online connections multimillion-dollar companies such as Facebook, Google, Amazon, YouTube, Zappos, Realtor.com, Zillow, eBay, and more have no brick and mortar storefronts. They conduct their business purely online.

Many businesses have adapted to these new technologies and incorporated them into their business plan and marketing strategies. What we have seen from recent surveys is that the homebuilding industry still has room for improvement. While some builders have evolved, others still rely on the standards and practices set many years ago.
Let's take a look at a few important facts related to the homebuilding industry:

- **More than 90 percent of home buyers start their home search online.**

  That is a large percentage of your exact market. Shoppers are also frequenting the website more often to research a potential purchase and to look for additional information during their entire sales cycle.

- **48 percent of the time, the very first step taken by a home buyer is to go online to research homes or information.**

  Think about that— almost half of the time, buyers will go directly to the web to find the information they want. Compare that to just three percent who pick up a newspaper. Does your marketing investment reflect this proportion?

- **Homebuilders determined that the highest quality leads come from their website.**

  Online customers are more informed, serious shoppers who can make a quicker decision than walk-in traffic. Specifically, online customers who have been qualified and well taken care of tend to write a contract 30 percent of the time.

- **The faster you follow up with a customer, the more likely s/he is to make a purchase.**

  When a customer receives a fast and courteous response to an online request, the conversion rate increases dramatically. This is not easily accomplished by the traditional onsite sales agent.

- **Builders are not allocating enough marketing dollars to online sources to keep up with the demand.**

  Studies reflect a major lack of marketing dollars allocated to online marketing. Similar studies also show that the amount spent for online marketing will continue to increase in the years ahead.

- **Less than 15 percent of builders have a dedicated person to handle leads from online sources.**

  Leads are coming in over the web with little to no conversions because builders are not handling them quickly or effectively. A large segment of the market is undervalued.

- **50 percent of the time, a new lead gets no response from a sales executive.**

  Recent secret shops of new home sales executives show that the current state of follow-up practices is not what it should be. In fact, the lack of follow up is now an epidemic. **Less than 10 percent of the secret shops show more than three contacts with a buyer!** Builders must anticipate the increase of online shoppers and the growing expectations for these potential home buyers.

A recent survey conducted for the National Association of Home Builders' Institute of Residential Marketing by Harris Interactive suggests that builders need to boost their online-marketing dollar allocations and develop their internet presence. By utilizing internet listing services and improving online content on builder's websites, they will be able to take advantage of the increased online traffic and benefit from greater sales activity. The potential for a higher volume of quality leads through these channels would allow them to focus the remainder of their marketing resources on what they identify as the most effective, offline marketing tools.

This study also revealed alarming trends in the lack of online contact between the builder and the consumer. Builders are missing an easy opportunity to connect with their target audience and would benefit by having a staff person dedicated to handling internet leads. According to the study, only eight percent of participating builders claimed to have a dedicated internet salesperson to handle leads.

This revealing study is screaming one thing loud and clear: Most homebuilders are not taking advantage of the large amount of people searching online for their new homes.

The bad news is, many builders do not have a great presence online and don't follow up with their leads.

So what is the good news? Well, many builders do not have a great presence online and don't follow up with their leads. That's good news for you, because their failure presents a huge opportunity for those who are willing to channel their marketing efforts to be where the buyers are. In addition, builders who initiate a program to effectively manage online customers will be well ahead of their competition.

Your Next Homebuyer

Builders need to take note. The next generation of homebuyers will look much different than what you have seen to date. Your Baby Boomer buyers did not grow up with technology. They used to prefer phone calls and face-to-face interaction. But even that's changing, as more of them are texting and "Facebooking" to communicate.

More than half of internet users ages 19 to 29 use the web to research housing. Those who have grown up in the Information Age will be more likely to start a search online. Are you ready for those customers?

The new generation of buyers, Gen X and Gen Y, are much different than their elders, and they make up roughly 36 percent of the population, so take note. These young buyers prefer anonymity. They would much rather research new home information online and communicate via e-mail, text, and online chat. They do not want to commit to any product or builder until they have the information they need. This generation expects easy access to the information they want. And why would they not? They experience this type of service for a multitude of other products, so they understandably expect the same results when they shop for a new home.

The Gen X crowd, born between 1965 and 1979, has been in the market for a few years and created the shift in expectations. The older members of the Gen Y crowd, born between 1980 and 2000, are starting to make their presence known in the market and, in the next few years, will comprise a large portion of your buyers.

The real question is: Will you evolve to deliver on this new buyer's expectations? The same old song and dance does not work anymore.

With an average gap of 24 years between those buying or selling real estate and those who represent them, will you be able to speak their tech savvy language when they come to you looking for a home? Let's face it, there is a huge difference between what they call a "digital native" versus a "digital immigrant".

How do you know if you are one of these immigrants? If you were born before 1970, there is a good chance you are. You know what it is like to use a typewriter, you remember buying your first Motorola brick phone, and you probably saw the fax machine make its way into the office. You are also a professional communicator and you know you have to stay on top of the latest technology and communication methods used by this new crowd. So here are a few tips to get to know Echo Boomers—the offspring of Baby Boomers—and what they are looking for when it comes to buying a home.

BE FOUND

We all know the stats—9 out of 10 home buyers start their searches online. Be found where they are looking! Establish your social community and treat it like your child. Feed it, dress it up, and take it places! Don't just set up a Facebook, LinkedIn, or Twitter account and let it sit there unattended. Nurture your social community and the Echo Boomers will notice you. Post your homes online! There are plenty of reputable listing sites ready to take your listing and get them sold! No longer does the rule "if you build it, they will come" apply, but rather "if you put it online, maintain and tweak it, they will come". Yeah, not as catchy, but the point is, the search starts online. Will buyers find you there?

BE SMART

With 94 percent of Echo Boomers using their cell phones to surf the web and send e-mails, a smartphone will keep you in the game! **Loose the dumb phone** and use your new iPhone—or smartphone of choice—to your advantage. You can send e-mails, text messages, photos, and videos, and connect with all of these new social networking sites at the touch of a fingertip. If you don't have a smartphone, stop reading this blog, go get one, and then we can talk (or maybe text?).

BE TEXTY

Get your texting fingers primed and ready. Don't be surprised if an Echo Boomer asks you to "text" them the details on a home or listing. Eighty percent say their cell phone is their "lifeline" and **would rather text than talk**. Be ready to respond to a text in a timely manner, which means no more chicken pecking! I know that for some of you this really chaps your hide. You might call your pubescent teenager on the cell phone that you pay for, leave them a message asking them where they are, and they text you back, "What do you want, mom/dad?" Well, this new generation is more responsive and comfortable using their thumbs than their mouths. Their punishment will be oversized thumbs and an early onset of carpal tunnel syndrome. **So who will have the last laugh?**

BE SPEEDY

Echo Boomers are accustomed to getting responses at the speed of light. When they e-mail you, call you, text you, Facebook you, they expect a response—and fast. In his book, "Grown Up Digital", Don Tapscott says it right—**the "Net Gen" has a 'need for speed'.** They have no idea what it is like to wait around; this is an immediate gratification generation.

Echo Boomers are adults now, not kids, and they want to be taken seriously and given the BEST customer service you have to give! Let's face it, this generation has high expectations of what this world should be like (especially with their first home). Who better to make that happen for them than you? No need to be discouraged because they want a trusted advisor. You actually have the competitive edge over your Echo Boomer counterparts, but you must be able to speak their language.

The Next Step

An Online Sales Program has an extremely high return on investment. The largest initial expense is a website; however, once it is up and running, the continuing cost to maintain the site is fairly low.

Online advertising is much more affordable than almost all traditional marketing sources. It is scalable and allows a builder to track the response and adjust the message with the simple click of a mouse.

The cost of e-mail marketing is low compared to other forms of direct marketing. When you examine the cost-versus-benefit ratio, there should be nothing holding you back from starting an Online Sales Program.

This manual was created for builders at any point in this process. Whether you are completely new to the world of the internet or already have an online presence, you will be able to apply the concepts in this manual to further your reach online and to stay in touch with the thousands of consumers shopping for a new home every day. Sales and Marketing Managers can use this book as a reference guide for implementation and improvement. Current Online Sales Counselors can use this manual to fine-tune their program. Owners and Managers can review the strategies and apply them to their businesses.

Regardless of which category you fall into, an investment of time and energy into this new online market is guaranteed to do one thing—increase your sales!

CHAPTER SUMMARY

If most of your potential customers are starting their search for a new home online, then a good portion of your marketing and advertising budget needs to be allocated to online marketing. Many builders mismanage their online customers and undervalue this medium. There is a reason so many builders are moving 40 to 50 percent of their advertising budget online and setting up the position of the Online Sales Counselor. They invest heavily in their online marketing because they recognize the value of their online customers.

Chapter Two

THE ONLINE
SALES FORMULA

Ingredients for a successful online sales program

How are you handling your leads now? If you are like most builders, you provide either slow or no response to leads from your website. So, you purchased this manual to either implement or improve your Online Sales Program.

About now, you might be asking, "Is it really worth the effort and time it takes to implement this program?" I can tell you from experience that you will see tremendous success both in total sales numbers and in contracts once you put this program in effect.

When I work with builders to implement the Online Sales Program, many are excited (and often surprised) with the results. Previously, they may have been responding to the e-mail requests or forwarding the requests to the onsite agent, but they were not seeing positive results because they had only implemented portions of the Online Sales Program. What you must understand from the beginning is that this program can achieve tremendous success, but only if you implement every step of the Online Sales Formula. While you may be able to drive traffic to your website and convert browsers to a lead, you won't have a high conversion rate without a detailed follow-up process and a dedicated individual managing those leads.

Let's Do the Numbers

Most builders have the same questions about the success rate of an Online Sales Program. How many leads do you get each month? How many of those are converted to an appointment? How many appointments end up on contract? What are your statistics…etc…etc…etc.?

Below, I am sharing the numbers I have seen personally and what many other successful programs have experienced. Keep in mind that every market and builder is different. So, use these statistics as benchmarks, understanding that your numbers may vary slightly.

1-3%—Leads captured from online sources

You have many sources to drive traffic. What most builders use to determine this statistic is the number of new unique visits each month; not the total "hits" or even return visits. It is important to determine how many new users you attracted and how many of those requested further information. Use Google analytics or work with your webmaster to easily access these statistics. They should be able to install the software to track this for you.

A lead is qualified as one individual who submitted a request or called in directly from an online source. Many sources are included, but only the total unique visitor stat from your website should be used as the number to get your ratio. This is the easiest way to measure overall conversion.

20-25%—Leads converted to appointments

The total leads are from both online sources and incoming phone calls. The conversion ratio is based on appointments that are kept, not appointments scheduled but not kept. [Side note: While some appointments that are set will not be kept, in most cases, an 85% appointment kept ratio is what you should expect.]

30-35%—Appointments that write a contract

This number is based on leads that go on an appointment, write a contract, and close on the home. You will see some contracts fall through, so do not count the totals until the sale is closed.

5-10%—Increase in overall sales

You can expect to see an increase in the first year of this successful program. This does not take into consideration additional sales that are generated from a stronger web presence. It is hard to truly determine direct sources from the internet.

20-25%—Total sales generated by this program

You can expect to see a good portion of sales generated through this program. Keep in mind that these are additional sales or sales that you will not lose to your competition. You might have had some of these sales before, but now you will be sure to keep these numbers high.

Here is a visual graph to help you understand the Online Sales Program and the funnel of leads converted to a contract.

HOME SHOPPERS
90+% Use the Internet

ONLINE VISITORS
1-3% Submit Request

INTERNET LEAD
20-25% Schedule

APPOINTMENT
30-35% Write

CONTRACT

20-25% of Total Sales

Using the numbers above, you can estimate the amount of sales that will come from your Online Sales Program. If you have 10,000 visitors to your website in a month, you would convert between 6 and 12 contracts. Not a bad return.

In Chapter 13, I will outline ways to report and track these statistics so you can measure the success of this program.

Take the ratios presented here and use them to evaluate your current traffic and leads and then determine some potential numbers. You will be able to set some immediate goals and have a general idea of what is possible. If not, take some time and compile your numbers. How many leads do you have coming in now? How many are converting to sales? How many visitors do you have coming to your site?

We have proven time and time again that, when builders implement this program, they increase their sales enough to more than cover the cost of the online sales counselor position, the online marketing, and website development. But it doesn't stop there. They also increase their profit margin and bottom line. If you don't have a serious game plan to capture online buyers, your competitors will take this program and build homes for your customers!

New Math For Builders

There is a new formula for builders. Let's look at some of the latest numbers:

90%—The percentage of your homebuyers who use the internet to research new homes

12 Weeks—The average time it takes for internet buyers to purchase a home

391%—The greater likelihood to convert a lead when you respond within a minute or less

50%+—The percentage of New Home Sales Executives who **DO NOT FOLLOW UP** with qualified buyers

All these numbers add up to a huge opportunity!

The home buyer pool has become very shallow and competition has increased for their shrinking business. Now, more than any other time in history, buyers are using the web to research their choices. Savvy buyers are being very strategic—narrowing their choices of homes and communities, disqualifying as they go, and using the internet as their power tool to gather information. They are shopping almost twice as long before their first appointment to a model home. Throw into the mix the current fuel costs. At $4 per gallon, families aren't jumping in the minivan for a leisurely drive from one new home community to the next.

As builders work their way up and out of "the dip", it is critical to invest in online marketing. It's a costly mistake not to take the time to set up a process to manage the leads they receive.

Potential customers are craving better on-demand information. They expect top-notch customer service while they are shopping. Don't underestimate them or take their inquiries lightly. The builder who shows them this courtesy in the beginning will come out ahead in the end.

Homebuilders' marketing dollars and mindsets will need to shift to this shopping phase to capture the buyer sooner—instead of waiting around for the "walk in". It makes sense to go where the buyers are, and right now they are online, trying to determine if you are the right fit.

Are you convinced yet? Great! Now here is a brief overview of what the Online Sales Program entails.

The Pieces of the Puzzle

An effective Online Sales Program consists of five parts. To see true results, all of the elements need to be working in conjunction with each other. I have talked with many builders who are "almost" there, but lack one or more of the elements to really pull it all together. You can have a robust website with online marketing driving traffic and loads of leads coming in, but if you lack a process to manage, follow up and turn those leads into contracts, it is not worth the time or money.

Here's a look at the Online Sales Formula and its components.

- **Website**—Your online sales center
- **Online Marketing**—Multiple sources driving traffic to your website.
- **(CRM) Lead Management System**—Manage, track, and follow up with leads.
- **Online Sales Counselor**—Position dedicated to follow up, qualifying and scheduling appointments.
- **Online Sales Process**—Your follow-up process is key to high conversion rates.

If you are building this program from the ground up, you should consider implementing it in a certain order. It does not make sense to hire an Online Sales Counselor if you do not have enough leads coming into your website. On the other hand, it takes time to build a successful Online Sales Program with maximum amount of conversions; so don't wait until you have "enough" leads to hire a dedicated person.

Now, let's take a look at the Online Sales Formula in detail.

Website

Your website—your virtual model home—is the foundation of your Online Sales Program. Without an effective website, you will not be able to capture the leads needed to drive this program and increase sales. Most of you will have a website already. Do a thorough review of your current site. Compare it those of the leading builders who are doing it right so you can get ideas of what you might be missing. I strongly recommend hiring a reputable and established web design firm to review the site with you and make recommendations or completely redesign your site. The bottom line, you probably need a complete overhaul or some major updating. Don't cheap out on the most effective tool to attract new buyers. I will review in depth the necessary components of a successful builder's site in Chapter 3.

Online Marketing

Online marketing includes pay-per-click, search engine optimization, and third-party referral sites such as Newhomesource.com, Realtor.com, and Newhomesdirectory.com

There are also many local online advertising media and free sources such as craigslist. This is how you drive those qualified buyers to your site. Not only is this media targeted, but it is also inexpensive compared to traditional advertising and marketing. You can run a robust pay-per-click campaign for a fraction of the cost of print advertising in your local paper. I will review these options in detail in Chapter 4.

Lead Management System

The Lead Management System or CRM is the web-based software used to store your leads in a database. It automatically funnels the leads from online sources, eliminating manual entry. It also automates follow-up tasks. There are few very solid programs from which to choose. Using a Lead Management Program is essential. It will save the OSC and Sales Executive time and allow him or her to focus on sales instead of administration. It also serves as a great accountability tool for management to work with the team.

Online Sales Counselor

This is the essential piece of the puzzle. You could have everything else in the program, but without a dedicated salesperson to properly qualify and set the appointments, you will not see the high conversion ratios.

I will review the key benefits and requirements for an Online Sales Counselor in Chapter 6.

Online Sales Process

The Online Sales Process is similar to the New Home Sales Process in that the main goal is to follow up, qualify, and set appointments. The big difference is that the online version is initially done with an internet and phone shopper instead of a shake-hands-and-sit-down shopper.

By establishing a powerful process, you can handle a higher volume of leads and make sure that everyone receives top-notch customer service. I will review the steps of the Online Sales Process in detail in Chapter 7.

Collaboration

If your sales and marketing departments are not on board, you won't see true success. Onsite sales agents tend to resist at first, but once they see the benefits, the OSC will likely be their new best friend and they will treat the appointments like gold. Success will be determined by the excitement and effort displayed from the top down.

We will review all of these components in detail in the coming chapters. Keep in mind, however, that you will not see the increase in sales overnight. From the ground up, it will take about three to six months to implement a comprehensive Online Sales Program and another three to six months to see the true results. That's almost a year. That should be great motivation to get started today! By starting now, you will get a head start on your competition and be leading the way before they even know what hit them.

10 Reasons Why Your Current Online Sales Program Is Failing

All too often, I encounter Online Sales Programs that aren't running on all cylinders. When I talk with builders about the possibility of a 20 percent conversion rate from leads to appointments, many people will say, "How is that possible? We have an Online Sales Counselor and we just can't seem to get there."

This is when you need to look intently at your process and perform a checkup on your program. Here are some of the most common reasons we see an Online Sales Program underperforming:

Wrong Person—This position requires someone with the right drive, ambition, and organizational skills. They don't have to be a computer geek, but they do need to understand computers and programs. They also have to be motivated to pick up the phone and dial for dollars, plus be an e-mail wiz.

No or Low Support From Leadership—Does the manager even know what the OSC does? What about the owner? Sometimes, this position ends up as the redheaded stepchild. Not quite sales, not quite marketing. Make sure your Online Sales Counselor is deeply integrated into the sales team and recognized for sales that come from appointments.

Not Enough Leads—You can't just drop in a person and expect your leads to magically increase. You have to generate leads from every source possible; SEO, SEM, PPC, third-party listing services, and more. Spend some money to drive traffic and watch your appointment schedule fill up.

Holes in the Lead Funnel—Do the numbers on your website still ring the onsite sales agent's phone? If so, you are missing opportunities. In most phone shops, we see onsite sales agents answering about half of the calls! Don't let the best leads go unmanaged. All new leads, both by phone and e-mail, should go directly to the OSC. I have some clients who even direct the numbers on their signs directly to the OSC team.

No Defined Process—It takes a consistent and persistent process to succeed with online selling. You can't just shoot from the hip and expect a steady flow of results. Online prospects require a unique process with the sole goal of setting an appointment. Make sure you have that process defined and that everyone understands why this process is essential. The last thing you need is confusion on the part of the site agents as to why it's important to treat online sales leads like VIP visitors.

CRM is Non-existent—Are you using some Excel spreadsheet you created and Outlook reminders to manage your leads? The right CRM can save you literally thousands of hours and allow you to manage your leads more effectively. Having no CRM, or an outdated inefficient CRM, can cost you a lot of sales. Prospecting is tough and generating appointments is no easy task. Don't send your OSC to a gunfight with an empty squirt gun.

Rewarded for the Wrong Activities—Success is not about tasks. It's about getting appointments and closing sales. Make sure the bonus structure rewards the right activities. This position is not a butterflies and rainbows customer service role. Your OSC needs to have the drive to create that appointment and, ultimately, the sale. They are not just there to make friends on the phone. A proper bonus structure can increase your appointments overnight!

Hand-off Process Falls Flat—Are you losing momentum after you set the appointment? Does the sales executive even contact the prospect before they visit? In our shops, the answer is usually, "No." Make sure that the onsite sales executive is both calling and e-mailing with an introduction and an appointment reminder. You should see at least an 80 percent appointment kept ratio if the hand-off process is done correctly.

A Divided Mind—Is your OSC the warranty person, too? Huge fail! We might as well just have them be the assistant to the manager while you're at it. Not gonna work, people. Trying to lump too many "other" tasks on their plate will remove their focus from the true task at hand—sales.

Telephobia—Call reluctance is epidemic. Yes, we call this position the ONLINE Sales Counselor, but most appointments are set over the phone. Make sure they know how to effectively communicate over the phone. The more people they connect with, the better chance they have for setting appointments. [In many cases, it takes 20 outbound calls to set just one appointment.]

BONUS REASON: Onsite Sales is "Not so hot"—Finally, it doesn't matter how good your OSC program is, or how many appointments you set. If you have a lousy sales team, the closings won't happen.

Some of these tips will deliver a quick fix, but most will require time and attention to get your OSC Program to the level that creates additional sales. It's easy to cherry pick the best leads and easiest customers, but it is a true art to get that "on-the-fence buyer" to take the next step. **Remember, 50 percent of your leads are going to buy a house from someone at some time.** Do everything you can to increase your chances of that "someone" being you.

CHAPTER SUMMARY

You will see an overall increase in sales by implementing this program. You will also retain sales that might otherwise be lost to your competition. For this to happen, you must incorporate all of the components of the Online Sales Program to see true results. Do not leave anything out.

Chapter Three

HOMEBUILDER'S
WEBSITE

The online sales center

Seth Godin, author of "Permission Marketing" makes this statement about a website, **"Your website should be 100 percent focused on signing up strangers to give you permission to market to them."** When I first read this, a light went on. It made me think of how we were presenting ourselves online. Of course, we had our floor plans, neighborhoods, financing calculators, and some feel-good info about our builder on our website, but what were we really doing to convert the thousands of browsers who were coming there each month into buyers?

One of the keys to creating a successful Online Sales Program is having an audience of potential buyers. Since it has been determined that 90+ percent of all home buyers conduct their new home search online, your website should be like a magnet, drawing these people to your little corner of the internet. Once they land there, your website becomes a substitute for your brick-and-mortar sales center. So, all of your important marketing information should be easily accessible to your customers at any time 24/7.

There are multiple books dedicated to the topic of website design and usability. I will focus on the industry standards and tested methods used by builders all over the nation. Most likely, you are in a position to implement some of these methods to increase your conversion rate from online customers and attract more buyers.

100% Focused on Gaining Permission

It is an interesting concept that has developed during the past couple of years. As media outlets and technology are changing, it is increasingly critical to start personal conversations with customers in order to break through all of the clutter. Permission marketing has become the new caveat and more businesses are focused on gaining permission from customers to market to them.

One of the benefits of focusing on gaining permission via your website is that the cost to implement this program is relatively low compared to other marketing and advertising avenues. In fact, you can capitalize on the internet traffic that is already coming to your site and use new ways to build them into a solid customer base. It is a much easier task to compel online browsers to take the next step and initiate communication than it is to try a shotgun advertising campaign to attract shoppers who may not even be considering a new home. Focus on the browsers who are one step away from becoming customers—browsers who are already on your website.

There are two ways to increase interaction from browsers on your website. First, provide valuable information that is easily accessible. Secondly, offer an incentive for your browsers to contact you.

It's Time to Build a New Virtual Model

What kind of an impression would you make if people searching for a new home showed up at your model home and you had no furniture, just a small desk in a dimly lit corner and weeds in the flowerbeds? When they asked for a brochure, a salesperson would hand them a crinkly piece of paper with the prices scribbled on it. I'm sure you wouldn't expect a return visit from them any time soon.

Sadly, this may be what's happening on your website. How many browsers abandon their online search after visiting your homepage because of the lack of information, complicated navigation, "under construction" pages, and poor or outdated design? If 90+ percent of new home buyers are starting their search online, then it is extremely likely that your website will be their first impression of you as a builder.

One of the things I've noticed more and more lately with builders is that when we look at all of the pieces of the puzzle to the Online Sales Program, one of the first things we look at is the website. And for many builders, my recommendation is that they need to create a new website. A good site should contain certain features, functionality, and updating—and that's going to cost money.

As soon as I say,"new website", I can see them start to cringe. Then I hear, "Oooh, I just don't want to spend any more money on that. We just redesigned it a year or two ago."

But look at the fundamental shift that has happened in consumer behavior. It used to be that your traffic walked into your model home, and this was their primary source of data gathering. Now, fewer people are coming into the model home—it's a quarter or less of what the traffic was before, yet online traffic has increased.

If you look at the numbers and cost it takes to keep model homes open for one month versus what a builder will spend in one to three years on their website—and compare those dollars to the traffic each attracts—there is a huge disconnect.

I'm not saying you should shut down your model homes. Buyers expect to see that, but investing more in your model home than in your online marketing is just a bad choice. Since most of the first visits for buyers happen on your website, make sure you are accurately representing yourself online. Ask yourself: **What kind of impression is my site making?** Does it accurately reflect the image I have in the community? Maybe you don't know...maybe you think you know. You must look at your site with a fresh—and objective—eye. Consider how your buyer would see it. Make sure that you have all of the pieces of the puzzle in their proper positions— and that they're accessible. Make it easy for them to find what they need and to navigate quickly. Anything that takes too many clicks or too long to upload is going to either frustrate your site's visitor or send them away.

Creating and maintaining a modern, user-friendly website is just as important as creating that perfect model home. When you are justifying your website design and ongoing investment, you need to put it on the same list of line items that you include with other operational costs. Steer clear of having to tighten up where it doesn't make sense. You always have to watch your money, but ultimately, customers are spending time on your website.

Internet years are like dog years. If your website is more than two years old, it's time to start thinking about a refresh or a revamp. And don't be tight with your money when it comes to a tool that makes a huge difference. If you were to pick just one marketing source in which to invest a good amount of your money, the hands-down choice should be your website. It can be used in so many different ways—lead generation being an essential one. The website is one of the best investments you can make—don't skimp. You'll pay the price in lost sales.

Builder Website "Must Haves"

Here is a great list of "Must Have" and "Nice to Have" elements for a homebuilder's website:

Must Have:

- Professional design
- Easy navigation
- Quick access to locations, neighborhoods, and floor plans (usually a search option is utilized)
- Supporting pages highlighting builder features such as design studio, warranties, and guarantees
- Financial calculation tools (one of the biggest questions for most home buyers)
- Highly detailed and printable floor plans
- Maps and directions
- Builder's story
- Support pages: testimonials, building process, latest news, promotions, etc.
- Noticeable "Contact Us" graphic or link on every page
- OSC marketing page (where you promote and encourage contact)
- E-mail newsletter sign-up (even if you aren't using it yet)
- Realtor relations page (a large portion of your business comes from these professionals)
- Customer service/warranty relations page
- Career section
- Blog for articles
- Social media channels (links to your Facebook, Twitter, Google+, LinkedIn)
- Mobile version/app

Nice to Have:

- Interactive floor plans (ability for customers to customize floor plans)
- Customer portfolio (customers can register and save floor plans, neighborhoods, etc.)
- Streaming video tours of homes or neighborhoods
- Priority/VIP list sign up for "Coming Soon" communities
- Live chat (managed by your OSC)
- Interactive plat maps for availability
- Customizable brochures to view, save, and print
- Area information and guides
- Videos (e.g., virtual tours) peppered throughout the site

Inventory Management

What is the one thing that browsers spend most of their time doing on your site? They are looking at your inventory, including available floor plans, communities, and move-in-ready homes. It is crucial that this information be kept up-to-date. You don't want to disappoint or frustrate an excited buyer who calls and finds out that the home listed on the site has been sold or the community has been closed out.

Make sure that you are able to access this information on your own and that the OSC or someone in the office is keeping it as current as possible.

Also, verify that your inventory can be "pushed" to the third-party sites that list them. With the proper system set up, you will only need to update the inventory in one place and the latest information will be sent automatically to the other sites via an XML (Extensible Markup Language) feed.

If you do not have this ability, you will be spending too much time updating your inventory in multiple places. Budget the extra money up front to make sure you are not spending unnecessary time administrating. In the end, you will save hundreds of hours of data entry.

Call to Action

As mentioned before, your website should be 100 percent focused on gaining permission from the browsers to market to them. You need to convert these browsers into buyers. This can be achieved by providing a specific call to action on every page. Here are some great examples of "calls to action:"

- Contact us
- Request information
- Schedule an appointment
- Request current pricing
- Ask the OSC a question
- Register for the builder online portfolio
- Sign up for the e-mail newsletter
- Request an eBrochure
- Priority registration for "coming soon" neighborhoods
- Realtor registration

Brainstorm ways to get customers to interact with you. What information do they want? What have they asked for most often in your previous interactions? Make sure that your "call to action" is clear and every page has some way for the customer to interact with you.

A standard conversion average to keep in mind is between .5 and 2 percent of your unique visitors. For example, if you have 1,000 unique visitors per month, you should expect between 5 and 20 people to contact you, sign up for an online portfolio, register for a newsletter, etc. This is just a standard to start with. Strive to get those conversion rates up as high as possible. Make it your goal to get between 2 and 5 percent. Consistently tweak and test to determine what works best.

Remember, focus on increasing those conversions. While it is good to drive as much traffic to your website as possible, sometimes all it takes is a slight change in wording or "call to action" to increase that conversion percentage—and usually that does not cost much. With only a slight increase in your conversion percentage, you can almost double the amount of leads you will receive!

Going Mobile: Mobile Websites

Are you "Third Screen Marketing" enabled?

For years, I have been asking "Do You Convert"? Now I have to ask, does your website convert for the mobile internet?

Internet-enabled phones hit today's market and gained popularity at an astonishing rate, resulting in a mobile internet boom. Hence, "third screen marketing", which refers to marketing to mobile devices. With this trend, we must now ask, **does my website provide a positive consumer experience on the mobile web?**

With the changing trend toward browsing on the go, your website needs to be useful in this fast-paced world of mobile browsing. If your site is slow to load, hard to read, and hard to browse on a smartphone, then you may be losing leads. The consumer needs are changing and you will have to change with them to keep these consumers engaged.

A vast majority of the world's population now has a mobile phone. In places like the United States, that translates to 9 out of 10 people. In the past year, more people in the U.S. accessed the internet using a mobile device than with a personal computer.

As smartphone devices multiply in the pockets of Americans, the face and pace of internet browsing is changing rapidly. This is an important shift for homebuilders to note—or be left behind. It is no longer an option to optimize for the mobile world. Either adapt to the hot technology or step aside for your competitors to fill your shoes.

For the most part, current builder websites are not optimized for the mobile world. Data needs to be pared down, easy to load, easier to navigate, and quick, quick, quick! Your standard website is most likely not compatible with viewing on a mobile device, like smartphones and tablets. In this hurry-up-and-do-it world, no one wants to wait around for a page to load on a mobile phone. You have seconds to keep them.

The key to mobile websites...keep it simple.

When devising a mobile website, you have some important factors to consider. First off, either use your current web designer to integrate your current site with your mobile site, or hire a reputable mobile website design company.

Drill down to the main features your customers are looking for—community, availability, special pricing, directions, contact information. Remember that your mobile audience is different than your desktop audience. Those on a mobile device want to get the information fast. They're on the move and you need to show you can keep up. They will not spend long periods of time browsing floor plans, reading details, and selecting options.

Take into consideration the environment. You have a small screen to make a big impact and present the important information. You may be battling with low lighting conditions, poor connectivity, different screen sizes and orientations, and multiple distractions. By keeping in mind the limitations your mobile users encounter, you will better equipped to design a site that is user friendly on the go.

The mobile internet is already here. Builders no longer can use the budget excuse as a reason not to add a mobile site to their short list of important marketing and sales tools.

Selecting a Website Designer

Have you determined where you are in the process? Is your website a digital dinosaur? Maybe you are just getting started. Or, you might have a decent website, but you need to take it to the next level—from good to great. Maybe you are at the top of your game, but want to implement some new ideas to increase traffic. No matter where you are, you need a well-qualified website design company to manage the aspects of the site that you can't.

Take note of these two important tips for selecting your new "best friend":

- Do not make the mistake of choosing the "cheapest" option. As I'm sure you know, this is one area in which you "get what you pay for". Usually, companies that offer a drastically lower price will either not be able to produce the results you are looking for or can't support your site as it grows and changes.
- Web design companies are a dime a dozen. They range from guys working out of their basements in the evening to highly specialized companies employing several people. The selection process will take some time and there are many fine companies from which to choose. No matter which one you select, make sure it has an extensive portfolio in the homebuilding industry. You don't want to be paying for someone's learning curve.

You can narrow down your choices of web design companies simply by asking to see their work. Once they show you their portfolio, you'll be able to make an informed selection. Are their sites attractive and easy to navigate? Do they include everything they should? Call some of their clients (not just the ones they tell you to call) and ask for their honest opinions. Look for multiple good references and sites that encompass everything you need. Just take the time to interview multiple companies and compare the benefits of each one.

Through my research, there are a few industry leaders that stand out and have large portfolios of homebuilder websites and online tools. In the past, I have listed these options here in the book. There have been two problems with this: 1) These options have the potential to change; and 2) The web development company a builder will choose is based on a lot of different factors, like budget, size, capabilities etc. So if you would like a recommendation based on your needs, just head over to www. doyouconvert.com and send an e-mail from the contact page.

CHAPTER SUMMARY

Your website is the equivalent of a "Virtual Model Home". Every potential buyer should have enough information to encourage further interaction. Your website should be 100 percent focused on converting browsers into buyers by gaining permission from browsers to consistently market to them. Make sure that your site is more than just an online brochure. Encourage interaction and place clear "calls to action" on every page.

Hire a reputable web development company with a professional portfolio of homebuilder websites. Since more than 90 percent of home buyers are starting their search online, make sure your website's presentation is prepared to impress them.

Chapter Four

ONLINE
MARKETING

Drive internet shoppers to your website

You have a beautiful website that is functional, showcases your homes, highlights your builder's benefits and encourages interaction from browsers. However, no matter how great your website is, unless you figure out how to get the online shoppers to it, you might as well not have a site at all. The largest mall can be constructed with all of the finest stores, but if it is in the middle of the desert with no sign or advertising asking shoppers to, "Come buy from us", the shopping center would be doomed to failure.

That old business adage about showing up if you want to succeed should be updated in today's web-savvy environment to read, "Show up in the search results if you want to succeed!" It's not enough anymore to simply have an online presence. It needs to be powerful.

Many homebuilders have not taken the next step in the development of their online marketing. They have a virtual sales center on the web, but nothing that tells shoppers the model is open. This process is referred to as online or internet marketing.

Surveys tell us that 90 percent of homebuyers are using online sources to do their research. Here are a few other stats you need to take into consideration:

- 47 percent of the time, turning on the computer and browsing online for homes or information about homes is the very first step a prospective buyer takes in the sales process.

- Over 40 percent of buyers say they actually found the home they wanted to purchase from an online source.
- A separate survey of builders revealed that the total budget allocated for online advertising was one-fifth of the overall budget while consumers spent one-half of their time using online media. This means that **builders need to start allocating more time and money to the one place where customers prefer to shop for new homes: the internet.**

Online marketing is comprised of many different avenues to drive the traffic to your site. Time and time again, it's proven itself to be one of the most cost-effective marketing methods. Plus, it is easy to track results of marketing sources and dollars spent.

Before I break down online marketing avenues, I will address the offline marketing of your website because it is a fundamental step in driving traffic to your site.

With all of the information and details you can post on a website, you must ensure that every potential lead, prospect, and customer you come into contact with knows you have a glorious wealth of information online. You must think of your website as a virtual sales center with all of the models, communities, floor plans, and information gathered in one place. An online shopper will greatly appreciate that you have consolidated all this for quick access 24/7.

It is easy to get the message out. On every piece of marketing material or advertisement, **INCLUDE YOUR WEBSITE ADDRESS!**

Take a few moments and list all of the marketing collateral you currently have. Use the following as a starting point:

- Business cards
- Brochures
- Sales flyers
- Floor plans
- Plats or site plans
- Billboards
- Directional signs
- Yard signs
- Service trucks
- House wrap
- Newspaper and other print advertising
- Radio advertising
- T.V. advertising
- Promotional items like pens and notepads

Put your website address everywhere and burn the image into the brain of your customer. Reprint your brochures, get new business cards, and put stickers on your plats. Just make sure www.yourwebsite.com is out there for all to see!

Online Marketing

There are several different ways to drive traffic to your website utilizing online marketing. We'll focus on the areas that are necessary for homebuilders and have proven effective.

This consists of the following:

- Search engine optimization
- Pay-per-click advertising
- Third-party referral sites (NewHomeSource.com, NewHomesDirectory. com, Realtor.com, Zillow.com, Trulia.com, etc.)
- Free listing services (craigslist)

- Unique pay services (banner ads, targeted social media advertising, local advertising, eBay classifieds)

I will give only brief overviews here of these online marketing options. If you would like further information, there are infinite books and websites dedicated to these topics. However, I will go into detail on how homebuilders can effectively use these services and identify the speed bumps to avoid while maneuvering through all of your choices.

Organic vs. Paid Search

The top performing online marketing sources are driven by the search results from search engines, such as Google, Yahoo, and Bing. The two primary methods used to gain targeted search traffic are pay-per-click advertising (also known as PPC) and organic search. Organic search is the natural result you see when typing in search terms. This form can be increased through Search Engine Optimization or SEO, which uses the rules of each search engine—and, yes, they don't all play by the same rules—to get your site higher in the search engine page results (SERPs). Let's examine these two avenues and note the pros and cons of each.

Organic Search

Organic search refers to the list of web pages returned as the result of a keyword or phrase entered into the browser window of a search engine. They are in order of the most relevant, as determined by the search engine's algorithms (a formula used to determine importance, relevance, and usefulness). I don't care what anyone promises you, no company can "buy" the top listing in the organic results. It's purely up to the search engine and how it determines which sites appear first for any given search term. Engines like Google regularly change up their algorithms so it's possible you could be high in the SERPs one day and disappear the next. A good SEO pro will keep on top of these changes.

Fig. 1 – Organic Search Results Location

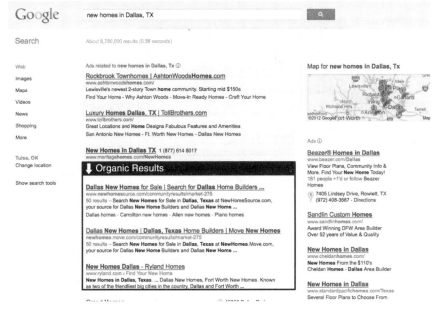

ORGANIC SEARCH RESULTS

Let's take a look at the basic differences between pay-per-click (PPC) and organic search engine optimization (SEO).

Pay-Per-Click Advertising

Advantages of Pay-Per-Click Advertising

- **Instant traffic**—After you set up your PPC campaign, the ads will usually start showing up within about ten minutes.

- **Highly targeted**—Easy to monitor which keywords bring visitors that actually convert and which ones don't. Then you can focus your ad budget on the highest converting keywords.

- **Powerful money-making tool**—One click could mean one home sold. A great source of marketing at a low cost.

Fig. 2 – Pay-Per-Click Ad Location

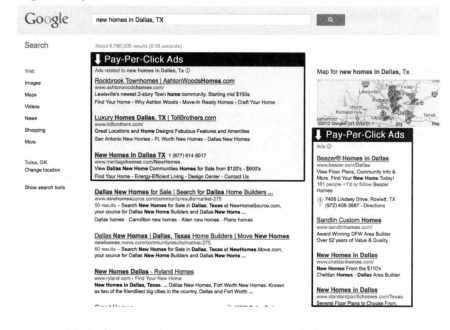

Disadvantages of Pay-Per-Click Advertising

- **Every click costs money**—When you stop paying, the visitors stop coming.
- **Must have a website that converts**—A good PPC campaign will drive targeted traffic to your site, but if your site doesn't convince those visitors to convert, you've wasted your money.
- **Growing competition**—The amount of competition for those top 10 ad spots grows every day. This drives up the cost per click over time.

Pay-per-click advertising is a great way to get traffic immediately. It's critical to have a website that effectively converts browsers into buyers in order to make more money than you spend. Once you establish that, however, PPC can be a powerful and profitable advertising method.

When you consider the cost of a home being sold, pay-per-click advertising will bring you a lot of bang for your buck! Something to look for is the competitiveness from the real estate industry and resale homes. More competition means higher-priced keywords. So, be sure to really zero in on specific keywords and consistently track your results so you know what's working.

One way to see that a campaign or keyword is successful is to utilize conversion tracking. This is a method by which you can monitor the conversion of a browser to a lead. For most homebuilders, conversion would be having a customer register online or fill out a contact form so that you ultimately capture their information. By placing a snippet of code on the registration or contact "Thank you" page, you can track when a customer registers after landing on your website by clicking on a specific keyword. This would then be counted as a "conversion." If this sounds complicated, there are many firms that specialize in establishing PPC advertising accounts and can handle the details for you. What you need to know is that it is necessary to track what works and what doesn't so you can adjust the dollars being allocated.

Search Engine Optimization

Another form of search engine marketing is called Search Engine Optimization or SEO. It is the method of increasing "natural" or "organic" search engine listings. These are the listings that come up in the main search engine results. Basically, SEO is marketing by appealing to the search engines to increase the relevance—and ultimately traffic—to your website.

SEO is concerned with improving the number and position of a site's listings in the organic search results. You want to be #1—or as close to it as possible—in the organic results for the new home searches that browsers are using.

Advantages of Organic Search

- **Clicks are free**—Unlike the people who come to you via PPC ads, the visitors that find you through organic search results are totally free, so there's a very high return on investment on those clicks.
- **More clicks**—More searchers click in the organic search results than in the PPC ads. In fact, studies show a **250 percent increase over pay-per-click**. A #1 ranking in organic will bring you more targeted traffic than paying for #1 placement via PPC.
- **More trust**—Most online surfers trust the search engine. When they see that it considers your site the #1 authority for their search term, many will inherently trust you. The implied validation of your site by the search engine makes it easier to convert those visitors into customers. **Studies show a 30% higher conversion rate from organic search results than PPC**.
- **Cheaper in the long run**—The initial investment in an organic search campaign depends on the competitiveness in your market. It is a long-term investment so you won't see immediate results, but by investing a little time and money in your SEO each month, you can gradually build up your site to attract free targeted traffic that will last long after you have paid—delivering a strong ROI (return on investment)!

Disadvantages of Organic Search

- **High ranking takes time**—You may start seeing noticeable traffic increases within a few weeks to a few months. It all depends on the competitiveness of your market.
- **The rules change**—Keeping up with the changes in the search engine's rules for ranking websites can be tedious. You are not guaranteed high ranking forever.
- **Requires investment in your website**—You'll need to commit more of your time to get good organic rankings. With PPC, you simply

drive visitors to a specific page and try to get them to convert. With organic search, you need good content that is useful to your visitors and portrays your company as the best builder in order to gain the search engines' attention.

There are many SEO strategies used, but usually include the following:

- Keyword research
- Paid and free website linking
- Search engine submission
- Content optimization
- Statistics analysis

SEO can often generate a good ROI. However, as the search engines are not paid for the traffic they send from organic search, the algorithms used can—and do—change regularly; there are no guarantees of success, either in the short or long term. Due to this lack of certainty, SEO is often compared to traditional public relations (PR) efforts (i.e., free publicity) with PPC advertising closer to traditional advertising.

Over the years, many professionals have asked me about how to get those first page rankings. For many of you, not a week goes by without some company e-mailing you with empty promises of attaining first page results for your website. No one can honestly make that guarantee. Search engines like Google and Yahoo! are far more sophisticated than any of these self-professed SEO wizards.

Balancing PPC Advertising and SEO

The best marketing strategy is striking a balance between both PPC and organic search. You can start driving traffic to your site now through pay-per-click while gradually building organic search rankings. As the site starts to rank highly for certain keywords in organic searches, you may decide to decrease your bids on those keywords on the PPC side.

Utilizing both of these methods is very cost effective and a homebuilder will see a high return on investment if the website is set up to convert this traffic.

Third-Party Referral Sites

This refers to the websites and portals set up specifically to advertise and drive traffic for new home builders. These sites are dedicated to finding targeted and qualified new home shoppers.

These sites include:

- **NewHomesDirectory.com**
- **NewHomeSource.com**
- **Move.com**
- **Realtor.com**
- **NewHomeGuide.com**
- **Homes.com**
- **Zillow.com**
- **Trulia.com**

More are emerging every day and there may even be regional sites that would be a good source. Nationally, these are the top performers and the best investment in any market. There are also crossover sites for traditional real estate that might be effective for listing completed or under-construction homes. These portal sites usually charge per community listed and might have options for featured listings.

Most of these sites will require your inventory and models to be sent in an XML "data feed" from your website. Usually, once you have this set up with one site, they can share this feed with the other advertising sites as well, which limits the amount of time required for data entry. (For more information, go back to "Inventory Management" in Chapter 3.)

All these choices can make it seem overwhelming. So, the best thing to do is to set a budget. Don't spend all of your money in one place. Instead, spread it out over multiple sites and see what works best. Usually, you will find that the amount of leads and contracts produced from these sites will far outweigh the cost. Also, keep in mind that a high percentage of people viewing these sites will just print off the directions and drive out to the site without ever contacting you from your website. That's just the nature of the system.

Since some sites work better in certain markets, testing and tracking is required to fine-tune your marketing budget over time. Keep ongoing statistics of leads produced from these sites and also the amount of appointments set and contracts converted.

These third-party referral sites also invest a great amount of time and money ensuring that they show up in the top positions of organic and sponsored listings in the search engines. If you are actively engaged in online marketing, you will potentially have your website accessible all over the first page of search engine results.

Free Listing and Classified Services

Online classifieds are a great avenue for listing your inventory and driving traffic. The services below are free or basic listings. You will see great results if you have special offers or promotions that will attract buyers. These sites consist of:

- Craigslist.org
- backpage.com
- HotPads.com
- LiveDeal.com
- Oodle.com
- Propsmart.com
- Vast.com

Personally, I have seen the results from Craigslist rival that of our PPC in both traffic and conversions. All this with no cost except the time it takes to create a compelling listing. I'm sure there are more out there and more being created every day. You will also find local listing services in your market.

Sometimes, listings can be time consuming. Free services like Postlets. com will help you create online flyers and automatically post to most of these sites.

Also, if you are using third-party referral sites like NewHomeSource.com, they will usually push your listings to many of the popular free sites as well. Check into that before you spend your time posting on these sites.

Unique Pay Services

Beyond the common listing services and advertising sources mentioned above, there are many unique sources and local listing services that you can discover in your own market. Some great places to start looking for additional advertising are:

- Facebook advertising
- Local *online* newspapers
- Local Home Builders Association
- Chamber of Commerce
- Banner ads for targeted sites
- eBay Classifieds
- Local city or state website portals

Opportunities will crawl out of the woodwork. The best way to find these sources is to start searching for homes as a customer would. Think of it this way: Instead of waiting for customers to drive to your model home site, you can take the initiative and advertise on websites that drive the traffic to you.

Where To Start With A Limited Budget

If this is all prompting a "Ca-CHING" sound in your head, don't listen. There are ways to achieve results with even a small budget. Here's a question I received from the marketing director of a small builder on the East Coast:

"I am dragging my builder (kicking and screaming) into this century with my marketing schedule, heavily revolved around reaching prospects online. This involves an immediate second release of their current website to include more methods to obtain consumer contact information. What advice do you have for a tech savvy marketing director starting a one-woman show from the ground floor up—oh yeah, and with a limited budget?"

This is a common question and there are so many things that are possible, but you MUST focus on what will net you the best results first! Then, once you have demonstrated a high ROI from these efforts, you will be able to champion for more of the budget and convince those Powers That Be of the massive potential of the internet. Here is how I would suggest starting your program.

- **Website first**—Make sure it has all of the information properly displayed and **strong calls to action on every page** (e.g., "Click here to register for our enewsletter", "Contact us for more details"). Work on converting the "low hanging fruit"—those who have already made it to your website. They just need the right nudge to take that step.
- **Online process (this is a close second)**—Implement your CRM and fine-tune your online sales process to increase conversion rates of leads. Keep detailed statistics to show your builder how much he spends per lead, per appointment, and per sale.
- **Tap into your database**—Develop a monthly newsletter to e-mail current prospects in your database. A little bit of time and $30 a month

for an e-mail marketing service like Constant Contact, AWeber, or MailChimp will go a long way.

- **SEO**—Increase your organic position on the search engines. This takes a little bit of time and money, so start now to gain the long-term benefit.
- **Supplement with PPC**—Start a targeted pay-per-click campaign on Google to drive immediate traffic. Commit to a specified amount to start. You can work with as little as $50 a month to test the waters.
- **Listing Portals**—List all or a portion of your inventory on the third-party listing services like NewHomeSource.com or NewHomesDirectory. com. Start with the ones that get the most traffic in your area.
- **In Your Spare Time**—Take advantage of the free and powerful social networking sites like Facebook, LinkedIn, and Twitter. Also get your blog going, post regularly, and distribute great content through your own site and multiple profiles on these strong networks.

The old question stands the test of time: How do you eat an elephant? *One bite at a time, people, one bite at a time.*

Procrastination is the Devil

Even though the web allows you to connect with your target market faster, you must remember that closings don't happen immediately. The actions or marketing initiatives you decide to implement now will not garner results immediately. When you sell a home, you don't enjoy the fruits of that labor for four to six months. Most new home sales take that long to build, complete, and close, and the closing is where everyone finally gets paid.

The same pattern holds true for your online marketing strategy. Just because you're ready to start your online marketing today doesn't mean you'll see an influx of new customers tomorrow. Deciding to create a new website, redesigning an existing one, or buying pay-per-click advertising today won't provide you with results, like closings, for about four to six months.

Consider a new website design. It takes about two to three months to complete the new site. Once it is "live," plan on another three months to start seeing a return on your investment (assuming you've invested in SEO and SEM) with new leads. Add another month to convert that lead into an appointment and then to a contract. So, on your calendar, you can expect at least a four- or five-month lag time between the launch of the site and a new sale—and that's if you started today. Once you invest the initial time in building the site, you set in motion a system to generate leads. Then, as you continue to maintain the site with fresh content and updates, you'll experience a steady, lead generating machine.

Any delay in the start of this initiative and a year could pass before you see results. **What are you waiting for? Take action now! Create a sense of urgency for implementing your new marketing program.**

Managing your calendar is extremely important, especially when it comes to your marketing initiatives, because those initiatives turn into sales and, ultimately, to closings.

The last thing you want is to contract a bad case of **"Analysis Paralysis".** This is what happens when you over-analyze the situation or try to make decisions by committee. Be bold and do whatever you can to move the needle in the right direction.

Newspaper Advertising: Are You Still Hanging On?

In many presentations, I ask the question, **"Is anyone here still advertising in the paper?"** Many hands creep up in response.

After presenting them the overwhelming evidence that this is not the best place to advertise homes for sale, there are still some diehards who cling to this medium as a viable source. The good news is that their population is smaller than in years past. However, I am perplexed at the percentage of advertising budgets that are still allocated to the newspaper.

At a recent conference, we were discussing this topic again with real estate company owners. Interested in getting more feedback, I posted a quick question on Facebook:

"Having a 'robust' discussion about newspaper advertising w/ broker owners. Still a lot of companies committing a large part of their budget to the paper. What would you tell them?"

Here are some of the responses:

"Numbers don't lie... take an objective look at the money out versus money in, then make your decision."

"Don't give money to people that write bad things about you!"

"Have you heard of an iPad? Let me show you something..."

"The lowest quality prospect comes from print media!"

"I'd ask them how they measure success of their print ads. Do they accept the anecdotal evidence from their sales offices? How much do they pay per acquisition? I guarantee they can make that metric drop like a rock if they diverted most of that budget to digital!"

"Measure to manage and look for other ways to give your sellers their marketing placebo. Sellers get excited when you tell them their listing will be in the newspaper because they know you're spending money to market their home—not because they really think that will sell it. The trouble comes in that most sellers also know that there is little to no fee for you to put their listing in the MLS... so you MUST go beyond that, but don't go for the low hanging fruit with newspapers."

"I think at this time in our economy, it's hard to say what works. 90% of people start shopping online, yet in some regions (yes) print pulled. Numbers don't lie. Most of our budget is online."

"Call me. We changed our marketing mix and our market share keeps increasing with rerouting dollars."

"We sell more than almost any competitor in LV and we don't advertise in the paper at all—online is where it is at!"

"As far as branding, I would show people how we were different by NOT being in the outdated print material. They could still use it in a presentation, but I would use it to show a buyer what not to do. Then take them online live and show them your presence on the web."

"Let the stats do the talking...."

"Here's how we do it: set up a dedicated URL for each channel including print. Then, track each channel against five indicators of quality: total website traffic, time on site, pages viewed, return visits, and opt-in conversion. Seeing the numbers in print will do more convincing in 5 minutes than 5 hours of trying to convince someone verbally that print is a terrible ROI."

"Newspapers are dying." (from an Executive Editor of a national magazine)

I wanted to include a primer on SEO practices from someone who truly understands this topic so I went to Jim Adams, author of "The Little Black Book of SEO Secrets". For those of you who want a crash course, check out his tips as a bonus at the end of the book.

CHAPTER SUMMARY

Online Marketing, combined with your website, is the anchor of your Online Sales Program. You must devote the time, energy, and money to ensure you are driving traffic to your site. Unless you are an online marketing professional, I suggest that you find a reputable web marketing firm to help you navigate through the search engines and tackle the other aspects of internet promotion. You will be amazed at the amount of traffic you can produce by implementing these marketing methods.

Chapter Five

LEAD
MANAGEMENT

Selecting the right software

The Online Sales Program is not complete without the Customer Relationship Management (CRM) system. Once you receive more than 25 leads per month, this becomes a necessity. Here is Wikipedia's definition of a CRM:

"**Customer relationship management (CRM)** encompasses the capabilities, methodologies and technologies that support an enterprise in managing customer relationships. The general purpose of CRM is to enable organizations to better manage their customers through the introduction of reliable systems, processes and procedures."

So basically, a CRM program is a tool used to capture customer data, categorize, prioritize, track, and communicate.

Do not rely on generic off-the-shelf software or basic office software to handle your leads. You will need to incorporate an industry specific CRM for your lead management activity. There are quite a few available that are specifically for homebuilders. They come ready to capture your leads from a variety of sources, including your website and third-party referral sites.

How Much?

These homebuilder CRM systems usually have a monthly fee associated with them, as well as the initial set-up fee. Many start at $500 per month and go up, depending on the number of users and/or communities involved.

Your Options

There are countless CRM tools on the market. Keep in mind, as with most technology providers, the quality, capabilities, and customer service have drastically changed over time. When this book was first published, I included a list of five of the top programs used by builders. Since then, two of them have all but vanished, one was sold, and only two have continued to innovate and solidify their position as an effective tool for builders. If you would like my recommendation based on your size, volume or number of users, just drop me a note on www.doyouconvert.com.

What Your CRM Should Do

As you evaluate CRMs for your company, look for certain features that are necessities and the extras that would be nice to have.

Must-Have Features:

✔ **Automatically import leads from the website and portals.**
Eliminating the manual data entry is a key timesaver. This is like hiring one-third of a person. I remember my first two months on the job as an OSC. I used an off-the-shelf, PC-based CRM to manage my contacts. At first, it was not an issue to enter the leads. I was excited that so many people wanted information and that I had so many opportunities. Fast-forward a month. I would cringe when an e-mail arrived. Why? I knew that one e-mail required me to manually enter the customer's information, set up a schedule, send an e-mail, set the next response, and so on. One contact would require up to eight steps for a follow-up. Multiply that times 100! Not to mention what it took for me to respond remotely. With that volume, it was nearly impossible!

Entering leads into a system manually is a time and labor-intensive process that wears on a salesperson's soul. Eventually, as more leads come in from successful online marketing, they will take longer to enter into the system and responses will not be timely. Without the speedy response that the customer is expecting, you will not experience the high conversion rates generally associated with online customers.

I quickly discovered that I needed to automate that process to free up my time. When we implemented a CRM system, I was able to focus more on generating new traffic and setting appointments. I could open up my CRM system and there would be five new customers on my screen—ready and waiting for a response. It was fantastic!

✔ Assign automated follow-up tasks.

You must have the ability to assign a set of tasks to each lead as it is qualified. Some systems will even assign them automatically based on registration information. If you receive more than 50 leads each month, then automatically assigning follow-up tasks is a must-have feature because you spend less time on administration. In addition, the tasks don't just tell you what to do and when, but also provide a way to easily complete the task using a click or two. For example, if you have a task scheduled to send an e-mail, you should be able to click on that task, open up the template, personalize the email, and send it off. If you can't do this in the matter of a few seconds, you are wasting valuable time.

✔ Cloud-based.

Do your online shoppers only e-mail you during business hours? Of course not. Then, hopefully, you will not just respond during business hours. By using a web-based lead management program that functions in the cloud computing world, you have the option to respond to leads while comfortably sitting at home in your pajamas! Web-based means that you are not just running a program on one physical hard drive, but that you have access to it from any computer with an internet connection. That's the wonderful convenience that the cloud gives you.

Any motivated OSC will take a few minutes in the evening to respond to a lead. As you should know by now, one of the keys to higher conversion is a timely response—even if it's a quick, "I got your e-mail and I'll get back with you in the morning" message. I have had several instances when I sent a personal response to a customer within minutes late in the evening. By using a cloud-based lead management program, you can provide exceptional customer service that will exceed your online shopper's expectations.

✔ **Be capable of reporting and tracking marketing sources, conversion rates, and activity.**

One of the main advantages of online marketing is that all of the activity can be tracked. Having a system that reports these statistics is key.

✔ **Maintain records and notes on each lead.**

Ongoing communication requires thorough notes so that you can identify a customer and recall specific details, no matter how much time has passed. A CRM tool keeps that information handy, so you don't have to search through e-mails or hand-written post-its to track it down. It is also crucial to pass this information on to the onsite agents when an appointment is set so they have more information on the buyer.

✔ **Provide a calendar for unique tasks, appointments, and follow-up activities.**

Once a lead has responded, you will schedule your communication on a customized timeline with a customized message. You must be able to set up tasks, events, and appointments for your lead.

✔ **Send a graphic-rich HTML or text e-mail.**

You need to have the ability to set up professionally looking, graphic-rich, branded e-mail newsletters to send to your leads. Almost all e-mail programs accept HTML e-mails and this could make a lasting impression on customers and prompt a positive response.

✔ **Track e-mail campaign statistics.**

Statistics track bounces, opens, click-throughs, and unsubscribes. These numbers can be used to monitor and gauge the success of programs and campaigns. Even though leads have requested information, there may come a time when they are out of the market area, so you should give them the option to unsubscribe easily. In fact, SPAM laws require that you provide this step.

✔ **Track customer usage on the website.**

It's great to find out who is opening your e-mails and clicking through to your website. You need to take that one step further with advanced website tracking. Using these analytics, you can learn how many times a customer has returned to your website, what pages they view, and how often. This is valuable intel and will be needed when scoring your leads and prioritizing who to follow up with and how.

✔ **Check for duplicate leads.**

You might receive multiple requests from multiple sources and communities. You do not want the same customer on three different follow-up campaigns. As your database grows, it will be harder for you to recognize who has already registered and who is a new lead. A CRM that automatically cross-checks contacts will help to eliminate duplicates.

✔ **It must be easy.**

I can't stress this enough. If your system is not easy or intuitive, your sales executives will not use it. Your CRM program is supposed to save you time and make you more efficient, not bog you down with extra steps, slow connections, or a cumbersome interface. It has to be "third grade easy" in order to create excitement around managing your tasks!

One thing you must take away from this chapter is to implement a CRM NOW! The sooner the better, because the longer you wait, the less effective this will be—not to mention the time it will take to import all of your old leads.

Selecting the Right CRM Partner

You have an important choice to make. Take your time, compare your options, and be sure to speak with customers who are actually using the program. Ask the companies to provide a list of builders who are using their software so you can get their feedback. Make an educated decision for the long term and plan ahead. It is never fun to try and then switch software with a database full of leads, notes, and records. Aim for increased leads and more active interest from online customers. Don't just plan for today and settle on the cheapest product.

Dave Clements, CEO of Lasso Data Systems, a leading provider of customer relationship management solutions geared specifically for builders, offered these insights and information on CRM.

CRM Is Your New Best Friend

Other than idiosyncratic and superstitious quirks, like wearing the same underwear from the grand opening until you make your first sale, there aren't too many secrets left in the new home sales process. There is change, constant change, and evolution as we all adapt to the new communication avenues present on the internet. But at its heart, selling a house is still selling a house—connect with a prospect, show off the property, do whatever it is you do to sell, and then close the deal.

For a long time, CRM software was one of the last and best-kept secrets in new home sales. As is often the case, the homebuilding industry took a while to understand, embrace, and adopt this new technology. Today, there is an accelerating trend among many developer and homebuilder sales teams. They are embracing CRM and realizing the benefits of having a centralized database of prospects and buyers leads that are accessible across their organizations.

Why employ CRM, and how can it benefit a sales team, and help convert leads and close contracts? Here are a few reasons why a robust CRM solution can become a sales team's new best friend.

CRM keeps information consistent and centralized. There are still many internet-friendly sales organizations that are still relying on outmoded, spreadsheet-based systems for tracking their leads. Information needs to be copied across multiple documents, increasing the likelihood for error and resulting in inconsistent, inaccurate, often outdated data.

With a CRM solution, a centralized database is created, and through the CRM, parties across the organization can update the same information in the same place. Departments can also share information more effectively about prospects or buyers—if a customer service rep has a conversation with a buyer about an amenity package, it can be noted in the customer record so that the salesperson is never out of the loop on any communication with his or her prospect.

More importantly, that database remains consistent and complete even as one community closes and the next project opens up. Many builders right now are facing difficulties selling out projects, moving those last few homes that will take unoccupied homes off the books. A CRM database can help by providing an instant "interest list" for new projects or existing projects that still have homes available. A quick e-mail blast to the entire database can reach those who may have recently resumed a new home search, providing fresh new leads from a database of those who may have once seemed like lost opportunities.

CRM enables effective follow-up. A CRM system is like an instant 'to-do' list for a sales agent each day—they can easily access an up-to-date, accurate, complete list of all of their prospects, as well as a listing of when each was last contacted. Using that information, sales professionals can determine who needs a phone call or an e-mail, who should make an appointment to come into the sales center, and who may be close to closing on a home. From a management perspective, CRM can help create a culture of accountability, as it can be used to track how each salesperson is progressing with their active leads. Managers can use this information to help facilitate the sales process and work individually with each salesperson for constructive coaching, and personal development growth.

CRM facilitates marketing. Today, a robust CRM system will serve double duty—it will provide an amazing resource for a sales team and a consistent lead database, it will also have e-mail marketing capabilities built in. This allows the marketing team to send messages directly to the lead database without having to employ a separate or external system; it also helps streamline the lead tracking process, as each e-mail sent will automatically be noted in automatically as a history item in each lead's profile record in the system. Sales professionals will know when each e-mail went out, which prospect opened or forwarded the e-mail, and the contents of each e-mail. This is invaluable information to have when performing follow-up calls.

CRM is more than just the best friend your real estate sales team ever had—it's the technology 'bridge' between old-school selling techniques and the rise of Web 2.0 and social media services. With CRM, no lead gets lost and no sale is missed—every piece of information that comes through the sales team can be documented and stored. It's an invaluable resource, and any sales team serious about converting leads should investigate it.

CHAPTER SUMMARY

Selecting the proper CRM is critical for your Online Sales Program. Without a program to manage your leads, you will not be able to properly follow up and convert the browsers into buyers. You will need to start using a CRM once you start creeping towards 25+ leads per month. Ultimately, this system will save you time and money while increasing sales.

Chapter Six

THE ONLINE
SALES COUNSELOR

A sales agent for the information age

The Online Sales Counselor (OSC)—a.k.a. Internet Concierge, Online Community Specialist, New Home Consultant, etc.—is the person who ties together the whole Online Sales Program. This position represents a new breed of sales agent—one who uses technology, e-mail, and phone skills to qualify leads, set appointments, and communicate the builder's message. Without a dedicated individual, your leads will go stale and eventually find their way to your competitors.

Most sales managers ask, "Why do I need a dedicated person to handle the leads from our website? We have salespeople who are paid to do that." Primarily, it's because most onsite sales agents are too busy with the walk-in traffic and current deals to be concerned with qualifying a lead and doing persistent follow-up with "potential" buyers. Just think of the laundry list of responsibilities onsite agents have for each home they sell. And these responsibilities are necessary to hold the deal together so they can get paid. They feel like they must spend their time concentrating on the buyers at their doorstep rather than those who might exist in the virtual space of the online world. Responding to and following up with leads ranks low on the priority list. This attitude (good or bad) is understandable.

The reality is, bad onsite agents suck at follow-up with new inbound leads and good ones just can't find time to give them the attention they need. Logistically, it is just not possible. If a good sales executive is doing their job, then they will likely be in appointments with prospects all day on Saturday—not answering phone calls or responding to e-mails. So what happens? The prospect moves on until they find someone who will respond. Or, they might just drive out to your site and get poor or no service because the sales executive is focused on other clients.

Instead of fighting an uphill battle to change how an onsite agent thinks, concentrate one individual's—the OSC's—energy on qualifying and converting all the leads for all your communities and pay them a bonus on their success.

Key Benefits of an OSC

There are four key benefits to implementing a dedicated person to handle your leads:

1. Immediate response will increase your conversion rate.
2. Unbiased qualification speeds up the home search.
3. Continual follow-up builds trust before the initial meeting.
4. A focus on setting appointments accelerates the sales process.

Immediate Response

Speed of the first response is the number one factor that will increase the number of conversions from a lead to a sale. A survey of 25 million data points by Lead 360 showed that following up with a lead in one minute or less of receiving the inquiry increases your chances of conversion by 391 percent. Once your response time moves past 30 minutes, your chances decrease almost 100 times. The numbers don't lie. Online shoppers expect immediate follow-up. Think about your own online shopping experience. Just order something from Amazon, make a transaction at your bank, download a song from iTunes, use live chat for support—you'll get the picture of how we as consumers are being trained to expect immediate response.

Prompt follow-up is critical to conversion, and many sales executives just don't have the capacity to effectively handle the job. An OSC, however, has the time and resources to meet or exceed these expectations and will almost always do a better job than the traditional agent.

Unbiased Qualification

An OSC is only concerned about qualifying customers and setting appointments at the community that best fits their needs. This style of informational selling puts the customer at ease and is seen as a true benefit. One thing that slows down the buying process is when leads go to a neighborhood that doesn't match their needs. When this happens, most onsite sales agents are not concerned about finding them the right home or community unless *they* can sell it to them. An OSC will set qualified appointments at the perfect community based on each customer's needs, giving the onsite agent a better opportunity to close the deal.

Consistent Follow-up

By responding quickly, sending customized e-mails, and establishing a line of communication based on permission, the OSC familiarizes the customer with the builder and the builder's main selling features. By the time this prospect visits the sales agent at the community, they feel like old friends. In fact, most customers have had five to seven encounters with the OSC—including e-mails, phone calls, and multiple website visits—before stepping foot onsite. This build-up of trust increases the likelihood of a sale. A survey from the National Association of Sales Executives reveals that 80 percent of sales are made between the fifth and twelfth contact. Compare those statistics with our own results from secret shops that show only three percent of sales executives send more than two e-mails and call more than once to an online prospect. What are the other 97 percent doing to cultivate prospects??

In addition, a sales agent is three times more likely to write a contract with a lead referred by the OSC than with walk-in traffic. They also have a higher tendency to write those contracts on the first visit. Isn't this a more efficient use of everyone's time?

Focus on Setting Appointments

As Myers Barnes states, "New home sales is all about the acceleration business." An intense focus on setting the appointment speeds up the sales process and will take the buyer "out of the market." One of the biggest challenges when working with online shoppers is getting them out from behind the safety of their computer and into your model home. By starting a one-to-one communication and using well-crafted e-mails and scripts, an OSC will motivate them to visit the onsite agent in the model. They can sell without "selling," the whole time weaving a message of uniqueness, urgency, and value into their communications. It is the job of the OSC to prospect and deliver "sales ready" leads to the onsite team.

I hope that by now you see the value of having a dedicated OSC. For those of you who still need proof, just look at what all the national builders are doing. They have implemented online sales programs to capture the leads and they have a team of OSCs handling these leads. It is obviously working for them. In fact, as the market becomes more competitive, builders are starting to take notice and implement these programs to convert more browsers into buyers.

The OSC is a Prospecting Machine

I heard a "business definition" that made me stop in my tracks.

Why? Because it applies DIRECTLY to the role of Online Sales Counselors.

The definition was of the word "prospecting." Simple enough, right? From a business perspective, it's defined as "finding new potential customers who have the ability, authority and willingness to purchase." All good things, right?

Think about it this way: at any given time, there is a certain percentage of the population looking to purchase a new home in your area. From there, a percentage of those folks will respond to your builder's promotional information—either by submitting an online lead or calling directly.

At this point, you're officially in PROSPECTING mode—and the good news is that the entire strategy for success can be boiled down into a few simple steps:

1. Start QUALIFYING prospects.

Your first job is to find out if a potential customer is a "true prospect" or not. That's pretty simple; just start a conversation—either offline or online—and proceed with qualifying questions such as area, timeframe, authority, wants/needs and financing. The longer you've been in business, the easier it'll be to pick up on the signs for whether a customer is the real deal or not. Many of your "leads" may not respond at all, and that's fine. You're looking for the ones that do.

2. Good information = Good business.

Once you've whittled down your prospect list to the truly interested customer base, your next task is to provide them with quality information. Your goal is two-fold—to both build value to the potential client in your presentation and to weave your primary selling points into the conversation. Above all else, have your questions prepared, which will make it easier to listen to your prospect's specific wants and needs.

3. Follow-up—and be persistent.

Don't be impatient. Home-buying decisions are among the most important in peoples' lives, and they take time. Just because a prospective customer doesn't call back immediately doesn't mean that they never will. Like any good sales associate, just do your absolute best to stay in touch and provide the right amount and quality of information. A sale is a moving target, and your job is to keep "firing away" until each target is in a position to buy—because then they'll think of you first.

4. Go for the appointment.

There's only one logical place to go from here—and that's asking for the personal, face-to-face appointment. As the saying goes, "if you can't SITE the prospect, you can't WRITE the contract." Think about it. Would YOU make one of the most important financial decisions of your life without even meeting a salesperson or company face to face? It's absolutely crucial to get each prospect in front of a living, caring sales executive— and your homes—to get them to take the next step.

It all starts with a pile of leads, and it's our job to:

1. Narrow the list to a subset of true buyers as quickly as possible.
2. Steer them to the right community, right home, and right decision.
3. Always see "the big picture"—not just setting appointments, but nurturing prospects along the entire sales cycle.

Sounds fairly simple, right? That's because it is.

All you need to do is get out there and start PROSPECTING—just like the definition.

OSC Qualifications and Characteristics

Think of an OSC as another sales agent. You need someone with the same propensity and drive for helping customers, but with a burning desire to succeed in setting appointments, as opposed to "closing the deal." However, the same closing techniques used for a sale can be used to "close" the appointment. In fact, only someone who has the courage to ask for the appointment **(every time)** will truly be successful. Many leads will have a laundry list of objections as to why they don't want to visit a community, give their e-mail address, receive your newsletter, or simply want to "think about it."

To have an OSC who is comfortable responding to these situations, you need a person who handles objections well, is willing to continuously work on self-improvement, and is eager to learn valuable scripts and techniques that will overcome the common objections, whether they arrive via e-mail or over the phone.

Many sales managers say to me, "It is hard to find a sales-oriented person who has a technology background." That's fine. I understand that, but you don't need a computer geek. You need a salesperson.

Once you have a process in place, almost anyone with decent computer skills can manage this program. Don't expect your OSC to handle the website development, search engine optimization, marketing, and/or the e-mail campaign programs. It is truly hard to find an individual who has both strong sales skills and strong website development and marketing skills. Also, with a high volume of leads, they will simply not have time to focus on these other areas.

Here is an ideal list of qualities to look for in an OSC:

- **Sales background**—An OSC is a salesperson first.
- **Strong computer skills**—Most of the OSC's job functions are conducted on a computer. Your candidate must be familiar with utilizing CRM programs and comfortable conducting business online.
- **Excellent phone skills**—When a lead responds, it is usually by phone. There is rarely any face-to-face selling.

- **Pleasant demeanor and great people skills**—Your OSC must be a natural when interacting with all types of people.
- **E-mail composition skills**—Most communication is handled through e-mail conversations, so your OSC must be able to respond professionally as a representative of your company.
- **Motivated by commission**—This is where salespeople excel, right? An OSC must be excited about the endless opportunities this profession offers.

OSC Job Functions

A dedicated OSC is ultimately responsible for handling all incoming leads. Even if you are only receiving a small amount of leads right now, there should be one person handling those leads quickly and efficiently. If you are a smaller builder with 100 leads or less, you can give the OSC additional responsibilities to help justify a full-time position. As you grow, you can adjust responsibilities accordingly. Keep in mind, the OSC must have the right tools and process (we'll discuss this later) in order to handle the high lead volume. You can expect an OSC to be able to handle, on average, about 200 to 250 leads per month before you will need to hire additional support. The higher the lead volume, the less ancillary work you can expect to be accomplished by this person.

Most common OSC job functions include:

- Respond quickly and personally to all online leads
- Handle all incoming phone leads
- Provide persistent and targeted follow-up
- Qualify the lead based on individual wants and needs
- Set and schedule appointments for onsite sales agents
- Maintain database of leads with updated information and customer notes
- Track and report on conversion statistics

Secondary functions that most OSCs can handle, if the workload permits, include:

- Update and maintain inventory on website and third-party referral sites
- Conduct e-mail marketing campaigns
- Manage or track search engine marketing
- Continually research new sources for online advertising
- Maintain online marketing budget and conversion statistics

The OSC handles the lead until the appointment is set and then turns the responsibility over to the Onsite Sales Agent. Some relocation buyers may request more information from an OSC and want to go through the entire sales process with this person. Don't allow the process to go too far. Turn the lead over to the Onsite Sales Agent when the leads have been properly qualified.

Some builders have an OSC position set up to handle a lead all the way to closing. **That will limit the effectiveness of the online sales program and this position.** An OSC cannot properly handle any volume of leads if s/he is expected to work with a client through the whole process. If your OSC is spending time getting financing together, following up on paperwork, updating the buyer on the construction, putting out fires, and/or holding the deal together, s/he will not be able to respond quickly to the new leads arriving daily. This is, in essence, the Onsite Sales Agent's difficulty in handling leads and the reason the OSC position was created in the first place.

Unlike a busy salesperson, an OSC who is focused and trained will ask for the appointment every time and repeatedly "close" the lead until achieving the final result—the appointment. As you know, it is very unlikely that a sale will occur without the prospect visiting the neighborhood.

Think of all the calls and e-mails you will miss in one day when your OSC is selecting a homesite, preparing the contract, writing it up and closing the deal. This has happened to me a few times when I have manned a model home in one of our communities and I was not nearly as quick or effective.

Also, these additional duties will put an OSC in direct competition with the Onsite Sales Agent. This type of competition is unhealthy. If you keep it separate and have the OSC setting up appointments for the Onsite Sales Agents, everyone will be happy and you will sell more homes.

Hiring an Online Sales Counselor

You should use a similar process to hire an Online Sales Counselor as you do for an Onsite Sales Agent. There are a couple of tactics that will ensure you find the right person:

- Conduct the beginning phases using only e-mail correspondence to ensure prompt response.
- Require all resumes and questionnaires to be sent via e-mail.
- Conduct follow-up interview strictly by phone. Remember that buyers will never see the OSC. They will only talk with him or her by phone.
- Ask your candidate to answer sample e-mail requests based on information about your builder.

You will be able to eliminate about 95 percent of applicants by observing e-mail skills and promptness. As I said before, you are not looking for a computer geek, but you do need someone who is proficient in using computers and e-mail.

OSC Compensation & Salary Structure

One of the questions I am most frequently asked by a builder or sales manager is, "How much should I pay an OSC?" Usually, there is a slight cringe on their face because this is a new position that they will have to work into their budget. In fact, this is a large barrier for most builders. Typically, they are planning on hiring an administrative-type person who will handle the leads in addition to other tasks. They are planning on trying to keep the cost of salary as minimal as possible. That may work for smaller builders with fewer than 50 leads per month, but if you really want to convert more sales, you need to compensate the OSC in the same range as an Onsite Sales Agent.

Remember, this person has many of the same responsibilities as the Onsite Sales Agent, and will be increasing your sales 5 to 10 percent and ensuring that you do not lose sales to your competition. This is a new breed of salesperson and needs to be compensated accordingly. Just as you're willing to pay for a talented sales executive who can deliver results, a skilled OSC is not an expense but a revenue generator.

You may be questioning my recommendations, but I have seen the difference in conversion rates of the OSC who is an "information giver" and those professionals who focus on "closing appointments."

There are many ways to structure a compensation package for an OSC. You can either set up a straight commission package or a base salary plus commission. Commissions are to be paid per kept appointments and per contracts. By paying for appointments set and kept, the OSC will be motivated and focused on setting the appointment. This is the number one factor that leads to a sale. The bonus usually paid for an appointment when an OSC has a base salary is about $50 to $100, depending on volume. An OSC should also be paid a larger bonus for every appointment that turns into a contract. This ranges from $200 to $300.

Determining a salary structure is complicated and based on many factors that vary for each builder, such as the cost of living in that area and the job responsibilities of an OSC. Ultimately, you need to make sure the

OSC is continually motivated by the commission structure and has a fair compensation that's equal to an onsite sales agent.

Do not take the bonus out of the Onsite Sales Agent's commission. This breeds contempt for the OSC and will taint the appointments. The OSC should be every Onsite Sales Agent's best friend. They should treat the appointments from the OSC like a Solid Gold, A++++, Super Hot Lead.

Over time, as the program grows, you will need to revisit the pay structure to confirm its fairness. Also, there could be times where an OSC is not pulling his or her weight. You should be able to determine job effectiveness through tracking and reporting. I will review measuring the effectiveness of your program in Chapter 13.

OSC Work Schedule

I am always asked what hours an OSC should keep. Just as Onsite Sales Agents are in the model when people are out looking, an OSC should be manning e-mail and phones when people are browsing online. Ironically, that is usually during normal business hours—with a higher concentration during lunch time. Because of the ability to work in the office or remotely, an OSC can respond to leads from any location with a high-speed internet connection.

The speed of the initial response greatly affects the conversion ratio. This requires an "on call" approach to this position. An OSC needs to be flexible and willing to answer the calls and e-mails promptly. In turn, the builder will need to take a flexible look at the hours in which an OSC is required to work.

Sample OSC Job Description

XYZ Homes is currently in search of an Online Sales Counselor who will manage our online sales and marketing initiatives. The position will respond to, qualify, and manage the leads and customer requests for new homes. The individual will report directly to the Sales Manager.

Primary Job Responsibilities:

- Respond to all e-mail and phone leads immediately
- Qualify the leads based on needs
- Provide consistent follow-up to online prospects with the goal of setting an appointment with the Onsite Sales Agent
- Provide information and marketing material to prospects
- Respond to the sales line and voicemail for leads
- Work with the prospect to determine the best community and floor plan
- Utilize lead management software
- Create and deliver ongoing e-mail campaigns
- Track and report on lead activity and sales conversion ratios
- Maintain website content
- Monitor third-party websites and online advertising
- Continually research the competition and their online activities
- Additional responsibilities as needed

Job Qualifications:

- Two years of sales and/or marketing experience
- Customer focused and personable
- Proven e-mail and phone communication skills
- Knowledge of computers, search engines, and online marketing avenues

- Sales contact management database experience
- Solid organizational, planning, and management skills
- Self-directed and able to maintain focus while working in an unstructured environment with nominal supervision
- Ability to multi-task and manage time well
- Must be able to learn and follow proven sales process

CHAPTER SUMMARY

Using your Onsite Sales Agents to manage leads does not work. It takes a dedicated person to manage leads professionally and increase conversion rates. You are looking for someone who is sales-oriented and proficient in using the computer. Make sure that the OSC is compensated in a similar range as traditional agents.

Chapter Seven

THE ONLINE
SALES PROCESS

Step-by-step to higher conversions and more sales

We spent the first part of this manual reviewing ways to drive traffic and convert browsers into leads. So, what do you do now that you have a lead—a qualified person waiting patiently for your response?

When I first started as an OSC, there was not much help out there that provided the details I was looking for regarding a follow-up process. I spent the first year developing and fine-tuning my own process so I could increase the conversion rates from a lead to a buyer. I did this by shopping online for homes. I requested brochures from homebuilders, filled out contact forms, called fellow OSCs, and more. To my dismay, my research showed that there were not many homebuilders with a good process. However, I was able to pull from the best and throw it into my own mix.

What you see in this chapter is a process that has been tested many times over by builders, large and small. Use this as a guideline so you don't have to spend time reinventing the wheel and recreating the message. Take this framework and create the customized message that reflects your builder's brand.

Keep in mind that, although it appears to be a step-by-step process, this is a flexible program. Some leads will require more frequent phone calls, some more frequent e-mails. If someone sends an e-mail requesting to view a home, then pick up the phone and call. In general, this is a good plan to follow to ensure that you remain in contact with your potential home buyers.

The goal of the follow-up is to invoke a response from the lead so you can determine what to do next. Should you receive a response, you will adjust the follow-up process to a customized timeframe based on the individual customer's needs. The type of follow-up will depend on the type of response you receive from the customer.

First, let's review one of the classic New Home Sales Processes developed by Myers Barnes.

1. Meet & Greet
2. Qualify
3. Present/Overview
4. Demonstrate
5. Select One
6. Objections
7. Close
8. Follow-up
9. Follow-through
10. Referrals

URGENCY

This is a time-tested method and guarantees success if an onsite sales agent puts these methods into practice.

The Online Sales Process focuses on the first portion of the New Home Sales Process and will often overlap, depending on the level of involvement needed with the customer. Let's take a look at how to apply the Online Sales Process once you have received a lead.

LEAD

Meet & Greet
- Immediate E-mail Auto Response
- Personalized E-mail Response
- First Phone Call

No Response

Customer Responds

Short-Term Follow-Up
- E-mail Process
- Second & Third Phone Call

Qualify
- Qualifying Questions By E-mail
- Qualifying Questions By Phone

Long-Term Follow-Up
- Monthly Email Newsletters
- Additional Phone Calls and E-mails

Select One
- Narrow Down the Search Based On Answers to Qualifying Questions

Set Appointment
- Use Closing Techniques
- Use Urgency

As you can see, the Online Sales Process begins the actual home sales process. By the time most leads go on their first appointment, they already have a floor plan in mind and are looking seriously at purchasing their new home.

Unlike the New Home Sales Process, your lead has a choice to either respond or not. For this reason, there are two potential avenues to pursue: one for those occasions when the customer responds and another if s/he does not. You will need to be flexible and adjust your process according to each lead. A lead may be traveling down the "No Response" track and will send an e-mail or call you. At this point, you would move the lead over to the "Customer Responds" track and start working the process.

Follow-up: Your First Customer Service Test

Motivational sales speaker Nicki Joy says. "Follow-Up is your first customer service test."

So many sales executives have trouble following up after a motivated buyer has graced their doorstep. With that being the case, one can only assume that all of those internet and phone leads are not getting the royal treatment they deserve.

Buyers are more than a little reluctant right now to walk through that door, considering the tough economic climate. But they are still shopping! Add that to an already busy schedule full of soccer games, dance recitals, and limited family time, and it becomes obvious why doing their initial research online has become so prevalent. Your new customers are using the internet to shop, research, compare, and narrow down their choices. Ultimately, they use the process of elimination to narrow down their selection to an average of two to three builders or homes. If you make this shortlist, they'll probably reach out to you digitally and ask those final comparison questions.

It is at this critical moment that you have an opportunity to gain—or lose—a customer. You are being tested. How you follow-up will set the standard for both you and your company. Do you follow-up immediately? Do you follow-up professionally? Do you follow-up in a friendly and helpful manner? Consider these questions and then ask yourself if you would pass or fail the follow-up test. Remember, this is not a pass or fail test, but an opportunity to improve your process and the results.

I know that managing your current clients as well as new leads is time consuming. But I guarantee that if you respond in a timely, friendly, and consistent fashion, you will pass the customer service test and convert more of those Internet shoppers into satisfied customers.

Meet & Greet

This first step in the sales process is the key to setting the right tone. An immediate response by e-mail will help increase the conversion rates of your leads. As mentioned earlier, surveys show that a response within the first minute increases your conversion rate by 391 percent. Even waiting 30 minutes will reduce your chances by 100 times. Speed of the first response is probably the most critical piece of this puzzle. I recommend an auto response that is personal and lets customers know you have received their information and will be in touch soon. However, this does not count as your first response. The first response should be your personalized e-mail and phone call. Obviously, you will not be able to respond immediately all the time. An auto response will buy you a little time; but if you want to be successful, you must respond with lightning speed.

Determine the customer's needs as best as possible from the information they provided. Craft a personalized e-mail answering any questions they asked and asking further qualifying questions. Send this personalized response within minutes.

If customers include their phone numbers, look at the quality of each lead before you call. If they are asking for specific information or have asked a direct question, go ahead and call immediately.

For the Customer Who Responds

1. Qualify

This phase of the process includes segmentation of the lead and further qualifying questions. Sometimes, you will be able to qualify a lead from the information request. However, most of the time, it is a non-descript request or the customers do not know exactly what they want. In most cases, you should start the qualification process based on the information you have received, verify what they have sent so far, and ask further questions to really pinpoint their needs, desire, and potential to buy.

The five key components of qualification are:

1. Area
2. Timeframe
3. Authority
4. Financial resources
5. Wants, needs, desires

Here are some great examples of qualifying questions you can use on the phone or in your e-mails:

- Do you have a specific area or community in mind for your new home?
- Do you have a timeframe in mind for your upcoming move?
- Who will be enjoying this new home with you?
- Do you have a specific investment range in mind for your new home?
- What size are you considering for your new home?

I've also included more examples of scripts to integrate into your follow-up process later in this manual.

2. Select One

This step is critical. Once customers respond and are interested in finding the perfect home, you will need to help them determine the best fit. They may already be qualified for a certain area or need help to decide on an area or community. No matter where they are in the decision-making process, you will have access to all the communities and homes that are available and can match them to the one that best matches their needs. Customers will value your unbiased opinion and trust the recommendations that you make. By not being locked into one neighborhood, you will be able to narrow down their choices and make the selection process easier for them.

This choice contributes greatly to the conversion rate once they go on appointment. They will not be second-guessing their decision because they know you have listened to their needs and determined that this is the right area and community. When you have that info, you can transition to the Setting Appointment stage.

3. Set the Appointment

Seizing the opportunity to set an appointment is absolutely essential. The key is to be clear and ASK for what you want—in this case, usually one of the following:

- **An appointment** (best-case scenario—when prospects are ready to see properties)
- **Contact information** (ideal for first-time callers or other prospects who may need a little more coaxing through the sales cycle)
- **Opt-in permission** (allowing you to continue marketing directly to prospects about new properties, special opportunities, etc.)

Of course, you may also have the opportunity to ask deeper questions to more thoroughly qualify your prospects—many of whom may be stand-offish anyway. The more you're able to qualify each prospect, the more likely you are to be able to match them with the most appropriate available properties.

Like an estimated one in eight U.S. workers, one of my first jobs was at the local McDonald's. It wasn't that bad; I even spent quality time sporting the Hamburglar costume for the kids (which paid an extra 20 bucks, by the way). Plus, I got to spend most of my day in the drive-through window, which I enjoyed because: 1) I didn't have to touch the food; and 2) I got to interact with customers all day. All in all, a pretty sweet gig for a 15 year-old.

And I discovered genius behind the scenes of the drive-through window.

Behind the scenes, the company pioneered an incredibly successful, sales-spiking, prospect-pushing, margin-maximizing technique that Ray Kroc and his franchisees have mastered over the decades.

"Would you like FRIES with that?"

Embodied in a single phrase, this proven, powerful concept has entered the modern lexicon as the ultimate example of the up-sell, in which a salesperson can properly use a simple, subtle power of suggestion to convince customers to quickly take action and "get a deal" on their purchase.

You've probably heard this phrase countless times at the order counter or drive-through window (at McDonald's and elsewhere). It's not by accident; the entire McDonald's empire is built on processes—the company spends millions of dollars a year on research and development in this area—and our ordering process was no different.

We were literally given "scripts" that quickly burned into our subconscious minds through sheer repetition: "Welcome to McDonald's; may I take your order?" or perhaps, "Would you like to try our new McRib sandwich today?"

I quickly realized that the most powerful scripts by far were the "up-sell" scripts—"How about a hot apple pie?" or maybe "Can I Super Size that for you?" We learned what Mr. Kroc and his team knew: if you ask a customer to try (or to buy) something new, they'll often say, "Yes."

That's why we NEVER finished an order without asking for an up-sell. And when I saw how successful the strategy was, it just made the process easier and easier. The up-sell is achieved by just acknowledging human nature and using it to your competitive advantage; most customers like to be friendly, agreeable and not seen as "rocking the boat" or inflexible in social situations.

The "OSC Up-Sell"—ASK for the appointment, contact information or more!

Be ready to respond to common prospect objections. The more questions you ask, the more objections you will receive. Even after you've mastered the art of up-selling, you need to be ready to deal with at least occasional rejection. For example, I always made it a point to ask something like, "Have you had a chance to visit one of our model homes in _____ community." Often, I would hear, "No, thanks—we're just looking right now" or some other common diversionary reflex, but I was always ready with scripts to overcome those objections and more. And the up-selling cycle continues...

Is all this difficult, nerve-wracking and harder than it sounds here? Of course, it is! One of the main reasons you aren't asking for the appointment already is because of fear. Just keep in mind what IBM founder Thomas J. Watson famously said about perseverance in business: "If you want to succeed, double your failure rate."

And remember, if a 15-year-old in a Hamburglar costume can do it, you can, too.

4. Just Ask

Once you have determined a good fit for your customer, start the process for setting the appointment. If you can perfect this skill, you will be rich. This is the one area in which many OSCs falter. This phase of the process can be compared to the closing phase in the New Home Sales Process.

Many OSCs will not ask for the appointment unless customers seem like they are interested. That's unfortunate because this should be the ultimate goal of the follow-up process. You have to ask for the appointment. Don't be pushy; be sensitive to the needs of your customers. They will have objections such as picking a time to visit. You will need to overcome those objections and help them commit to a time to view the community or floor plan. There are several ways to ask for the appointment or encourage the interaction from a customer that will lead to an appointment. You will find useful scripts on setting the appointment in Chapters 8 and 9. If you establish urgency and provide great information, then setting the appointment will be the next natural step for you and your customer.

For the Customer Who Doesn't Respond

1. Short-term Follow-up

This phase of the process focuses on the personal short-term follow-up. It includes scheduled phone calls and e-mails along with any information the customer has requested. If customers do not respond to you immediately, you will put them on an auto follow-up campaign via e-mail (see Chapter 8). If customers do respond, you will need to set an individual follow-up schedule based on their needs. E-mail is a great tool, but do not be afraid to use the phone. Most appointments will be set over the phone and you can learn much more about the customer's needs in a shorter period of time. Make sure the customer knows you are only a phone call away.

All browsers who submit their information—either from your website or from another source—should be placed on an auto follow-up schedule. This is a high touch process with multiple contacts by e-mail and phone within one month. We will review this process in detail in the following chapter.

Once this process is complete, you will place the lead on "Follow-up Complete" status and send the monthly e-mail blast to all customers and include the additional personal e-mails and calls.

Now, this may look like a lot of work, but it isn't, as long as you have a system in place to handle it. If you don't have one yet, GET ONE! If you had 100 leads per month, that could mean sending more than 600 e-mails! The key here is to remember that you are a salesperson, not an administrator. Set up a system and use it!

2. Long-term Follow-up

Depending on the status of the lead, this phase is necessary to stay in contact with the customer over a longer period of time. Studies show the buying cycle for new homes is roughly 84 days with relocation buyers taking upward of six months to a year. Obviously, your goal is to get them on an appointment after the initial trigger point. By creating a long-term follow-up program, you will stay in touch with those who show interest, but do not respond immediately.

The best way to do this is by establishing an e-mail marketing campaign. I will review the components of the e-mail campaign in Chapter 10.

Visits versus Encounters

Another key benefit of an Online Sales Program is the number of encounters that customers have before they ever set foot in a model. An encounter can be a visit to the website, an e-mail or phone call from the OSC, follow-up e-mails and appointment confirmations. While not an actual visit to the model, these are essential steps that help breed familiarity between the customer and the builder, products, and the sales process. Familiarity will promote trust and trust will increase the likelihood of a sale.

When a lead is properly followed up, there are many personal encounters. Even if a lead wants to schedule an appointment on the first contact, he or she will have between three and five encounters prior to the in-person visit with the builder. This comes in the form of website visits, e-mails, phone calls, and information. These customers end up writing a contract

30 percent of the time—usually on the first actual "visit" to the model.

Staying Personal in the Digital Age

An Online Sales Counselor manages hundreds of leads per month by e-mail and phone. **Around 80 percent of these people won't even respond.** Of the ones who do, you will most likely never meet them face-to-face. The sheer volume of rejection and lack of personal interaction can lead to apathy if you are not careful.

You must constantly remind yourself that there are real people out there behind the e-mails and they need good information from someone they can trust. You must stay sharp. Every day and every lead is a new opportunity to help someone with one of the largest investments they will ever make. In a digital age, personal interaction is happening all the time—online, via cell phone, by e-mail. It is not just in person anymore. So take heart and know that, as an OSC, you are the first contact in one of the greatest decisions someone will make—building their new dream home. (Most of the book so far refers to the OSC in third person speaking more about them not to them but the above paragraph is speaking directly to an OSC).

CHAPTER SUMMARY

Selling homes online is a process. When you fine-tune this process, you will produce better results and higher conversion rates. Spending time preparing this process will pay off exponentially. It won't be long before every builder has a process like this established. Start now and stay ahead of your competition. Develop your process and experience the increase in sales you desire!

Chapter Eight

FOLLOW-UP
CAMPAIGN

Powerful scripts and examples that will invoke a
response

Every good sales process utilizes a script. The traditional New Home Sales
Process thrives on scripts. Memorizing these scripts allows a salesperson
to focus on selling and establishing rapport with a customer instead of
constantly trying to think of what to say next.

The Online Sales Process is no different. In fact, because of the higher
volume of prospects, it is essential that you have prepared scripts in many
forms to use and apply.

As most of your communication will be conducted by e-mail, this chapter
will focus on examples of phrasing that can be used for auto follow-up
campaigns and communication. I'm giving you many scripts that you can
piece together to create personalized e-mail sales letters to use in the
follow-up process.

As I mentioned in Chapter 7, there was little information available that
provided the details I was looking for on a follow-up process when I began
as an OSC. However, I was able to consolidate information, merge it with
original material, and create a message my builder could employ in our
follow-up e-mails.

This chapter is the result of that effort. As an OSC, this will be a valuable
chapter to reference as you develop your process. I encourage you to use

the phrases that work for you. Customize these templates so they mirror your company's values and mission. Craft a personalized message that reflects your builder's brand and, as with everything in this manual, make the scripts your own.

Keep in mind that this is a flexible program. Some leads will require more frequent phone calls or e-mails than what is listed here. In general, however, this is a good plan to follow to ensure that you remain in contact with your potential home buyers.

Most of these are generic enough to use in any market. Remember to personalize your approach for every lead, if possible. However, 60 to 75 percent of the time, a standardized follow-up campaign will work as you try to further qualify each lead. This is a great foundation from which to start because it allows you to build the program and follow-up campaigns as you go.

The goal of the follow-up is to invoke a response from the lead so you can determine what to do next. When you receive a response, you will adjust the follow-up process to a customized timeframe, based on the individual customer's needs. This process should be used when you do not receive a response from the customer.

Follow-Up Process

Here is a follow-up process to implement once you receive a lead online. I call this the "new market follow-up" as buyers are now in the market longer than they used to be. Many have a home they need to sell or reach out earlier in the shopping process. Because of this, we need to extend the number of times we reach out personally over that first year. Of course, they will still get the monthly e-blast or newsletter, but the personal e-mail or phone call will go a long way toward maintaining the connection. Think about it. How many prospects receive an e-mail touching base from a salesperson six months after the initial correspondence? What about after one year? Let's face it. Many salespeople aren't even working for the same company a year later. So here is the timing of this follow-up:

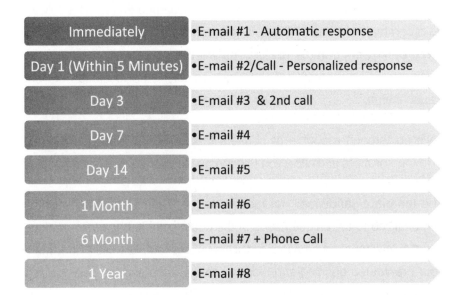

Immediately	•E-mail #1 - Automatic response
Day 1 (Within 5 Minutes)	•E-mail #2/Call - Personalized response
Day 3	•E-mail #3 & 2nd call
Day 7	•E-mail #4
Day 14	•E-mail #5
1 Month	•E-mail #6
6 Month	•E-mail #7 + Phone Call
1 Year	•E-mail #8

NOTE: You can always increase or decrease the follow-up, based on the needs of the customer. I also encourage a monthly follow-up email and phone call, but I don't include that in this process. That way we avoid what I call "task fatigue". We still send out specific email updates, but to all customers at a set time.

Let's Talk Templates

One of the critical components to a successful follow-up program is the e-mail template. Now, many people think that "template" is a dirty word. They might assume the message will sound canned or impersonal. Don't get me wrong. The "form-letter-brochure-copy-800-word-e-mail" templates are most definitely dirty. I would suggest you look at creating your e-mail templates in a different way. All I mean by "template" is something that is prepared in advance as a basis for future use. Don't reinvent the wheel every time you need to send an e-mail.

When you think about the e-mails you are currently sending, you will quickly realize that you use the same verbiage and phrases over and over again. So, in essence, you already have parts of your templates created. In working with many sales professionals, I have learned that with the follow-up program I recommend (five to seven contacts in the first month alone), if you don't work from templates, you will burn out quickly or dump the follow-up process completely because it's taking up too much of your valuable time.

Let's go through a couple of pointers that will simplify this part of the follow-up process and allow you to accomplish your goals more efficiently:

The template sandwich: I do recommend that every possible e-mail be personalized to the unique needs of the customer. That doesn't mean the entire e-mail must be personalized. Think of the template like a sandwich: Your pre-written opening and closing are the buns and the personalized sentence or two in the middle is the meat. The template sandwich shakes off the "form letter" feel and makes it all warm and fuzzy.

Build as you go: Trying to create your entire bank of 18 unique follow-up e-mail templates in one fell swoop is like writing a term paper the night before it is due—borderline impossible. I recommend starting the collection with your next follow-up e-mail. Spend time creating that template and save it for future use. Within two to three months, as you continue to refine it, you'll have everything you need for the future.

Keep it short: People don't read e-mails; they scan them. Keep them short, personal, and to the point—three paragraphs, with six to eight sentences total. When you start edging past that, it better be pretty darn informative or include information that they requested. Remember, we are not trying to sell a home by e-mail. The goal is to invoke a response, call-back, or visit.

Change it up: Are your template sandwiches getting stale? Revisit them every once in a while, add a new one into the mix and dump the old, dried-out ones. You need to think of five to seven different ways to communicate with a prospect so you will be memorable. Use lively words and short sentences.

At the end of the day, remember that the most important part of follow-up is just showing up. Template or not, most sales professionals quit after two follow-up attempts. By having a bundle of e-mail templates ready to go, you will be able to fire those off faster and more often than your competition.

Now, let's see what those e-mails and phone calls should look and sound like. In the first edition of this book, I laid out exact e-mail templates in this section; however, a problem occurred. As more and more builders used these scripts, more and more of the follow-up looked exactly the same. So I have removed the exact e-mails and instead included phrases that you can piece together. Remember, this is only a guideline, but one that I have found works very well.

Immediately—The Auto Response: E-mail #1

The goal of this e-mail is to let each customer know that you have received his or her request and that it is in the process of being reviewed. This step also gives you time to look over the customer's information and determine what kind of shopper this is. Understand that customers expect to receive an immediate reply because that's the norm today. They are accustomed to getting a quick response everywhere else online. So, it is no different when they submit a request to a homebuilder. Use phrasing in this e-mail like:

In order help you find the home of your dreams, I will contact you shortly to discuss your new home search.

You can expect a detailed response within one business day. If you prefer speaking with me by phone, please call 800-555-5555.

In the meantime, please visit our website at www.XYZHomes.com to browse our award-winning communities and homes.

Call attention to the strengths of your website. Tell them something they might have missed and give them the option to call. It is much easier to get the info you need via the phone. The main goal is to acknowledge their request and set the expectation.

Review the Lead and Rank

Now that you have the basic qualifying information, decide what type of shopper this is. It is pretty easy to determine that from the information he or she provides. When shoppers only give you a name and e-mail without including any details, asking a question, or adding comments, they might just be gathering information. If customers provide you with all of their information, three different phone numbers, and then ask where you are building a certain floor plan, they have clearly expressed genuine interest and will require a more intense follow-up.

If you have a lower lead volume, you might classify all of your leads as "A leads" and give them the royal treatment. However, it is important to focus first on the buyers asking specific questions or adding comments on their home search.

Most CRM systems have a ranking feature, so use that as a way to categorize online responses.

Day 1—The Personalized Response: E-mail #2

Now that you have reviewed the customer's request, formulate a response that is related to the request. The faster you can provide a personal response, the better conversion rates you will have. Responding as quickly as possible will kick-off the communication on the right foot and will increase your chances of connecting with that customer. Your goal is to respond within five minutes or less. Remember, the process is flexible and adaptable to provide the most rapid and effective response for each lead.

Most leads will require further qualification. You can use an introduction and closing that remains the same; then add the personalized response or qualifying questions in the middle. This saves time since, with 90 percent of the responses, you will use the same copy. Utilizing phrasing like:

> "My name is Mike Lyon. As the New Home Specialist for XYZ Homes, I am dedicated to providing fast and accurate information and helping people like you find the perfect home and community.
>
> I can be a valuable resource and answer all of your questions about a new home purchase.
>
> If you would like to schedule a tour at a specific community or have any questions, feel free to contact me at xxx-xxx-xxxx."

Of course, if they are asking a specific question about a floor plan or community, address that question in your response.

Day 1—The Phone Call

It is great when a lead provides a phone number. That is the best form of communication with a potential buyer because it enables you to ask a myriad of qualifying questions and accelerate the process. If a customer is asking a specific question or seems to be a highly qualified lead, call on the first day and then follow up call on the second or third day.

At times, getting the buyer on the phone is the challenge. If you end up going to voicemail, here are some sample messages you can leave.

> "Ms. Prospect, my name is Mike Lyon with XYZ Homes. I am following up with you on your request about community/home we received from _____. I recently sent you an e-mail with my contact information. Since I didn't reach you today, **I will call again tomorrow**. I think you'll be excited about what we have to offer you. You can also reach me directly at xxx-xxx-xxxx. That number again is xxx-xxx-xxxx. Thank you and have a great day."

After leaving the first message, change the status of the lead from the qualifying stage to the automatic follow-up stage. Be sure to follow up the next day with a message similar to this:

> "Ms. Prospect, this is Mike Lyon with XYZ Homes calling once again to talk about your new home search and to answer any questions you might have. I will be sure to follow up with you by e-mail, but please feel free to contact me at xxx-xxx-xxxx if you would like further information or to schedule a tour of our neighborhoods. Thanks and have a great day."

Remember, you are trying to invoke a response to better qualify this lead. If you are nervous about leaving messages, memorize and practice your script. Don't read from the page, but know what you want to say before the time comes. Nobody likes "uh-um" messages.

Day 3—Video E-mail

This is the part of the follow-up process where we get to use one of my favorite tools: video e-mail! Now, I have been sharing this little goodie since 2008. I think it is one of the most powerful communication tools a salesperson can use. In the hierarchy of communication, being able to see someone's face is a huge differentiator. Check out a few of the main reasons you should be geeking out right now over video e-mail:

- No one else is doing it. When was the last time someone sent you a video e-mail?
- It has a high impact. Because it is rare, people will think you are Steven Spielberg and will be impressed.
- You can communicate enthusiasm and humor with your facial expressions.
- It will guilt a customer into responding. Video e-mail has a large psychological weight. Your prospect will say, "Oh man, this person spent all this time sending me this. I have to respond!"

I personally recommend www.eyejot.com. Go for the Pro Plus version—don't cheap out. You can customize the e-mail template with your look and feel and also receive notifications when recipients open and view the video.

I am constantly surprised that more people don't use video e-mail. I present this tool to thousands of people every year and I rarely see any video e-mails or hear of widespread use. So I started asking "Why?" Come to find out, there are two main reasons:

Reason #1: People don't like the way they look on camera. My answer, GET OVER IT! That is just the way you look. Yes, it is uncomfortable at first, but the more you practice, the more comfortable you will get.

Reason #2: They don't have a webcam, don't understand the technology, can't figure it out, etc. And my response to that...SERIOUSLY? Webcams are cheap—www.eyejot.com Pro Plus is a whopping $99 a year. Find someone who can help you set it up and take action. If you want to be a better communicator and get more of your prospects to say yes, this is the tool!

So think of video e-mail as a voice-mail with your face. Highlight your services and let the customer know you are a valuable resource. Here is a sample message you could use.

Hello <prospect>

This is Mike with XYZ Homes. I'm sending you this quick video e-mail to let you know that I am here to answer any questions you might have. I know it can seem overwhelming looking for a new home. I want to make that easy for you.

It is my job to give you fast answers to your questions. Let's talk soon. You can call me at xxx-xxx-xxxx or just hit "Reply" to this video e-mail right now with your questions.

I'll be sure to continue to follow up with you. I hope to hear back from you soon.

Day 7—Follow Up: E-mail #4

This is a subtle follow-up reminding them of what they started out to do—research new homes online. Also, you will close the e-mail by asking for the appointment. Every time you follow up, ask for the appointment. You don't get paid until there is an appointment or a sale—so ask! What's the worst they could say? Here are some example phrases you can use.

> About a week ago, you were researching new homes online. I wanted to follow up and make sure you received the information that you need and address any further questions you may have.

> Because I work with all our communities, I can save you time and effort in your new home search.

Day 14—Follow-up: E-mail #5

Here is another e-mail example that highlights a feature of your builder and your services. I hear from many OSCs who tell me that the Day 7 and Day 14 e-mails generate a good amount of responses. Remember the study at the beginning. Less than three percent of sales executives follow up with more than two e-mails. Your persistence will start to pay off here. You might slide in financing questions that address other important aspects of their search.

> Do you have financing questions? Are you wondering how much you can afford?

> Do you have questions that need accurate, on-the-spot answers? If so, I'm here to help and can match you with the right home and put you in touch with our financing experts!

1 Month—Follow-up: E-mail #6

This is the "I give up e-mail" because it sends a message to the customer that you will ease up on your follow-up. Again, it is a great time to ask for an appointment and a response to the question, "How have I done?" I have seen many responses to this e-mail from buyers stating their status or asking for further information. I like to use a phrase like this:

> I take pride in providing the most extensive customer follow-up possible. It has been about a month since you initially contacted us and I want to be sure that I have met all of your expectations.

After sending this e-mail, the prospect will be placed in long-term follow-up and added to your monthly e-mail newsletter list. There are many reasons why they might not respond to your communication. Just because you don't get a response, it doesn't mean they are not interested. That is why you just keep going!

6 Month/1 Year—Follow-up

Who follows up with prospects after six months? What about a year? About three people in the world! OK that is a bit of an exaggeration, but does it pay off for those that do? Absolutely!

That is the good news for you. Now, the best way I have found to do this without getting "task fatigue" is to schedule 30 minutes on your calendar every month and pull a list of your leads segmented by creation date. For example, with all leads that are six months old, either create your follow-up email template or use one that is ready and send out the message to everyone (all good CRM systems have this functionality). This saves you from having to manually go in and complete each e-mail task individually, which will save you a lot of time. It also allows you to create a timely e-mail message for the clients and this will get you a better response.

The Hand-off Process

If everything goes as planned, you have the appointment with the lead to visit a community. Below you will find the hand-off process necessary to maintain momentum. The hand-off to the onsite sales executive is critical to complete with every appointment that is set. When using this process, your chance of achieving an 80 percent appointment-kept rate is almost guaranteed. [Note: For appointments that are scheduled for the same day, not all of the following handoff tasks may be needed.]

The OSC Handoff Responsibilities

Immediately	•Appointment Confirmation Email to Customer
Immediately	•Provide prospect information to onsite via email and call
Day Before	•Appointment Reminder Call
Day After	•Customer Courtesy Email/Call
Day After	•Appointment Verification with Onsite

The Transfer of Trust

Many times, you have shared multiple e-mails and phone calls with a prospect. This has allowed you to build trust (and a relationship) with that person. When the time comes to transfer that relationship, you may run into a few concerns presented by the prospect.

Here is a common statement I hear and an easy way to address the concern.

Prospect: "I thought I would be meeting with you at the community. Who is this new salesperson?"

OSC: "Ms. Prospect, as the Online Sales Counselor, I help customers, like you, to narrow down the many community choices and find the best fit. I know a lot about our 30 communities but <sales associate/s> is the expert on <his/her> community and can answer any questions you might have. I am going to give <sales agent's name> a call and share everything we have discussed. This way <agent name> will be able to focus only on the homes and topics of interest to you. In addition, s/hr will call you for an introduction. You will love working with <agent name>!"

[Note: By reinforcing the agent's name in your conversation, you help bridge the gap from online sales to site sales agents. The more you use the actual name of the agent, the more your prospect will feel comfortable with that agent before meeting.]

Use an appointment confirmation e-mail to send your lead the information on the area, directions, and contact numbers for the sales associate. This is also a good time to include financing information that they can get started on before the visit. Customers love this and it helps confirm the time and importance of the appointment. It also serves to transition them to the onsite agent.

Ms. Prospect,

We look forward to meeting with you on <day, date, time> at the <Community>! Below is the contact information for our onsite sales agent along with directions. If you have any questions in the meantime, please feel free to contact me. We'll see you soon!

Contact and Community information

Map and Directions

Financing Info

Transfer Prospect Information to Onsite

The goal of the hand-off to the sales agent is to maintain urgency and momentum with the prospect. Your relationship with the customer is paramount and you must transfer that knowledge to the onsite agent.

E-mailing the information is important, but a phone call completes the hand-off and allows you to convey the details of the conversation, along with the personality of the customer. This phone call is critical to recap the facts and communicate everything to the onsite agent.

After the appointment confirmation is sent and you've discussed the prospect with the onsite sales agent, send an e-mail to the onsite sales agent with the details of the prospect along with appointment time. As you have qualified this customer, be sure to include important facts about their needs along with their wants and desires.

Remember, with every prospect, there are those "hot buttons" that the onsite sales agent must be aware of.

Appointment Verification

In order to learn if your prospect kept their appointment and if they were a good fit for the community, it is the OSC's responsibility to follow up with the onsite sales agent. This verification is needed for your records, but will also determine who will be handling the follow-up for the upcoming weeks. Knowing that one out of three appointments turns into contracts, your onsite sales agent most likely will assume responsibility for follow-up to close the sale. You will want to perform periodic check-ins with the onsite sales agent through the next two weeks or until a contract is written.

The conversation with your onsite sales agent is important for your future success of appointment setting. Don't be afraid to ask or take note of something that you may have forgotten to uncover that would have been important information for the onsite sales agent to know prior to the appointment. The more you know, the more likely your appointments will show!

Appointment Missed E-mail

If a buyer does not show up for an appointment, send a quick follow-up via e-mail as well as a phone call to check in with them. The e-mail can go like this:

Sorry we missed you today. Our customers love our appointment process because it saves them time and allows us to focus one-on-one with them. If you get a chance, please call me at XXX-XXX-XXXX and I'll reschedule for a time that is more convenient for you. Thanks and I look forward to talking with you soon.

Monthly E-mail Newsletter

Once the auto-follow-up process is complete, you will move the lead into a monthly e-mail campaign for long-term follow-up. This is the e-mail newsletter highlighting monthly promotions, builder features, homebuilding advice, and much more. This step is part of your long-term plan for staying in touch with a contact.

Powerful Phrases

The e-mail examples we just reviewed are to be used as a guideline. You will need to customize them for your builder to reflect the following:

- Builder brand and message
- Promotions or incentives
- Service highlights
- Community-specific information
- Main selling points

Below are several scripts and phrases that you can use for inspiration or include in your e-mail messages. They can be building blocks for great e-mail content and compelling calls to action.

Introduction Phrases

I am here to assist you with any of our communities and floor plans. I can also answer your questions and provide additional information that could be helpful in your new home search.

It is my goal to provide you with the all of the information you will need to make an informed decision.

As your New Home Specialist, I am here to assist you and answer any questions. In order to help select your dream home, I will need some additional information...

I am here to save you time and money by assisting you with all of our communities in <location>. I will help you determine the best location and floorplan for you and your family.

Thank you for your recent interest in XYZ Homes. Please tell me what I can do to make your search for information easier.

Home Search/Qualifying Questions

Since I work with all of our communities, I can answer any questions you might have about the different areas, school districts, investment ranges, and included features.

It is my goal to understand your needs and help you select the perfect community. In order to assist you further, could you answer the following questions:

- When would you like to be in your new home?
- What investment range are you considering?
- Do you have a specific area in mind for your new home?

We have many areas, communities and floorplans to choose from. What is your preferred time frame? Do you need a new home right now or are you able to build from the ground up?

Follow-up Scripts

You recently requested information on XYZ Homes and I wanted to follow up with you. How is your new home search coming along? Is there additional information I can provide you?

It has been a few weeks since you requested information on XYZ Homes. I am here to answer any questions you have regarding your new home search in <location>.

It has been one month since your initial request for information on XYZ Homes. Please let me know how I can be of assistance and make your search easier.

Setting Appointments

Please call or e-mail me today to set up your visit with XYZ Homes. I can arrange the perfect time to view our beautiful model home and additional floorplans.

Feel free to contact me directly at 800-123-4567 for further information or to schedule a VIP tour at our communities.

I'd like to set up a time for you to stop by one of our XYZ model homes. I promise you an enjoyable and informative trip.

Many times, our model homes are quite busy. To be respectful of your time, I would like schedule a specific time so you won't be standing around "waiting your turn." Let me know what day and time will be convenient for you and I will handle all of the details.

If you would like to learn more about XYZ Homes or arrange a personal tour, please call me toll-free at 800-123-4567 or e-mail me at osc@XYZHomes.com.

I hope you've had a chance to review all the information I sent you on XYZ Homes. Whenever you are ready to see the neighborhood in person, I'll be happy to set that up for you.

Contact Me

I am available to assist you at any time. You can expect a detailed response to your e-mail requests and a prompt return call for any voice-mails.

If you have any questions or would like to schedule a visit, feel free to contact me be email, phone or even text me at directly at 919-123-4567. If you have any further questions about XYZ Homes, our communities, or floorplans, please do not hesitate to contact me directly. I look forward to assisting you with your new home search.

Better E-mail Subject Lines

Not only do the e-mails themselves require careful crafting in order to prompt a response, but the subject lines also matter. It is the subject line that pops into the inbox that prompts a prospect to open the e-mail, delete it, or mark it as junk.

Think about it. Do you open every single e-mail you get—especially if you know it is from someone who is trying to sell you something? Sometimes you look at the sender's name and other times, it's the subject line that catches your attention. There are ways, if you are that sales person, to get your e-mails opened (and hopefully read, clicked through, and responded to).

Start by beefing up your e-mail subject line. The subject line can be a deal breaker when it comes to e-mail campaigns. They can send you skyrocketing to super-stardom or to the depths of the trash folder with other unread e-mails or worse—the dreaded spam folder!

Let's check the stats:

MarketingSherpa.com recently conducted a survey of e-mail marketers, and 40 percent said that testing variations of their subject line had a high impact on their return on investment (ROI); 45 percent said subject line changes accounted for a medium ROI; and only 15 percent said that testing changes to their subject line resulted in a low ROI. So 85 percent of them saw a moderate to high ROI by trying different subject lines to gauge the difference that wording can make.

Here are a few tips to avoid the trash, stay out of spam, get read and get results.

- **Who are you?** It is vital that your readers know the e-mail is coming from you. If your e-mail causes confusion in the inbox, it will end up in the trash. The name of your company should be the first priority in every e-mail you send. Go into your e-mail settings and double check your "From" window and ensure your name as well as your company's name are set to be shown. For example, "From: Mike Lyon, XYZ Builder".
- **Make it personal.** If you know your readers personally or even a few facts about them, use that in your subject line. To catch their eye, put their first name in the subject line and it will set your e-mail apart from the others right there in the inbox. Rather than a subject line of "Your

Recent Home Search", you could type, "Mike—Your Personalized Home Search"

- **A matter of importance.** Always include as much important and pertinent information in your subject line as you can. If you send an e-mail about a specific home, or community or area, make sure that is featured.

- **Take it for a test drive.** Look through your past e-mail campaigns. Compare and contrast the winners and the losers. Keep an out for certain topics, styles, or trends that had popular open and conversion rates.

- **Be clear and concise.** Make it obvious what the e-mail is about in your subject line. If your reader has to click on your e-mail to understand what in the world you are talking about, your e-mail will fall into obscurity. This is your one shot to make it clear to readers what you want to say, so just say it!

- **Don't be a spammer. Spam is a four letter word** in the internet age. We don't like it, we don't want it, and our e-mail server knows this! They will filter you out of the inbox as soon as you click "Send". Avoid words such as free, stock, eBay, password, and mortgage, and do not exclaim anything! Keep exclamations away from your e-mails. Spam filters love them because readers do not like them.

How to Get Responses from "Generic" Leads

What do you do with all of the leads that only have an e-mail address and don't appear interested?

That's the million-dollar question and here's the million-dollar answer: **The goal of your follow-up program is to invoke a response from these prospects and build trust!** Not everyone will respond; that is to be expected. Your intention is to filter out the serious prospects (who are right for your business) and focus on moving them to the next stage.

Here are some tips to get a response from the leads that are best suited to you:

- Begin your e-mail with something directed at this specific person. When people think they are receiving a form letter, they tend to move on.
- Long e-mails are overwhelming to people, so keep it concise and specific. Use the lead's name to personalize it.
- Add a "Call Me Now" graphic or text in the center of the e-mail and make sure the person knows there's a live person ready to speak with them.
- Offer something they can't get from anyone else—limited time, "special incentives" are great. Set yourself up as the one they need to talk to, the one with something more to offer than anyone else.
- Remember the 80/20 rule. Don't lose sight of the 20 perfect matches because you are focusing on the 80 that might not ever contact you.
- Ask one strong, open-ended question at the end, giving them a reason to respond. An open-ended question means they can't answer with a yes or a no.
- Use video e-mail! I can't stress this enough. The visual aspect is an extremely powerful tool.

Shoppers are spending more time these days looking for a home— the research phase for an Internet buyer can be six months or longer. Just because they don't respond immediately doesn't mean they're not interested. It simply means they have not yet bought in. Follow up like they are an "A" lead and you stand a better chance of turning them into one. That will give you the edge over your competition and boost your conversion ratios.

Finally, be professionally persistent and personal. People buy from people they trust, and trust is built over time. You'll be surprised how many people will contact you a year or two later.

CHAPTER SUMMARY

Online Sales is a process. An OSC must provide a fast and courteous response, qualify the buyer, and schedule an appointment at the perfect neighborhood. You need to give unbiased information about your neighborhoods and communities, and should be a wealth of knowledge on your products, services, and process. No one can do what you do. This how-can-I-help-you attitude puts customers at ease and inspires them to open up with you. Remember, the point of these e-mail follow-up campaigns is to provoke a response. Ultimately, you want the lead to call or e-mail you and set the appointment. Hone your skills and increase your conversions every month. People are shopping 24/7/365 and you are there to help them make one of the largest investments of their lives. How exciting!

Chapter Nine

THE PHONE
IS YOUR FRIEND

Phone scripts for setting appointments

One of the most effective tools an OSC can use is the good ole' fashioned telephone. As much as you will use e-mail in the follow-up process, the telephone is the connection where most of the action occurs. A few minutes on the phone can cover the same ground as four or five e-mails shuffling back and forth with a customer. It is very important that the person you choose as an OSC has excellent phone skills and can think on his or her feet.

The goal is to have a customer call you in response to an e-mail or call in directly from the website or other advertising source. You absolutely, positively must answer every phone call to the greatest extent possible. Why? If you don't, the prospect most likely will not leave a message. It is a sad fact, but people just do not like to leave messages. When I first noticed this, I was surprised and thought, "Why wouldn't someone just leave a message?" Then, I remembered all of the times I had called a phone number I got from a "For Sale" sign in front of a home. If the Realtor did not answer, I would just hang up. My thought process for not leaving a message was:

- I am not that interested.
- I just want to know the price of the home. I'll get it another way.
- I don't want them to keep calling and pestering me.
- I don't want to play phone tag.

Here is one tactic I employ that can be successful when used correctly. When a customer calls while I am on the other line, I call back the number on the caller ID immediately (not more than a couple of minutes later). Then, when the customer answers, I say:

> This is Mike Lyon with XYZ Homes. I'm sorry that I was unable to transfer over in time when you called, but I was on the line with a customer. How may I help you today?

This generally receives a good response. I'm sure a customer would not appreciate a return call more than a couple of minutes past their initial call.

The bottom line is to answer every call possible. Of course, it's unreasonable to expect you to be able to answer every single one. Some will slip through cracks, but do your best. Think of every call as a potential sale. When I hear the phone ring, I also hear a "cha-ching" because I know someone is calling who is looking for a new home.

Selling Online Isn't Just About E-mail

When you hear the term "Online Sales", you think e-mail, e-mail, e-mail. But online is how your prospects find you; it doesn't mean that's the only way you should communicate.

The contact starts when you create an Online Sales program, but that's not where it ends. Almost all online sales that begin online will develop over the phone and finalize at the model home.

With e-mail, you may end up sending many more contacts back and forth in order to convey the information needed to get your prospect to an appointment. An e-mail conversation can last hours, days, or weeks. A single phone call can get all those questions out in the open and allow you to create urgency for an in person visit. This is why it's important not only to be articulate in your writing, but to work your phone presence as well.

To polish your phone performance anxieties, here are a few tips to follow when engaging with prospects on the phone.

If your phone rings, answer it.

Elementary, but it is absolutely necessary to answer the phone as quickly and frequently as possible. No matter how interested a lead is, they are not likely to leave a message. They want immediate answers and connection with a knowledgeable individual on the other line.

Funnel the calls to the right person.

You've invested marketing dollars to drive the traffic, so make sure all the numbers listed online go straight to your qualified online sales agent or someone who is dedicated to a fast response. Do not pass go, do not stop at the receptionist, do not let it go to a recording or through a maze of voicemail that takes far too long to navigate. You want your prospect to be welcomed with an immediate, live response.

Set the right voicemail message.

While we'd like to be on call 24/7, there will be moments when you just can't get to the phone. Make sure you have a voicemail set up with a message that offers a greeting and a name and gives the caller an estimated time for a return call. Be sure to express genuine interest in helping them with a home search.

Get their contact information.

No matter how positive, or negative, the prospect may sound over the phone, always get a name, phone number, and e-mail. Offer to send out a plat map, floorplan, or information on the homes you have been discussing so that you can get an e-mail. Too often, the phone call ends with nothing to show for it because you forgot to get the info.

Answer and ask questions.

After you answer the caller's initial questions, ask other qualifying questions such as area, price, timeframe, etc. Many times, a prospect thinks they know what they want but end up with something completely different. Take advantage of the opportunity to pre-qualify your prospects when you have them on the phone. They may call wanting one home, but fall for another because you did your job and got to the root of their needs.

Ask for the appointment.

A simple question, "Have you had the chance to visit our model home?" can go a long way. Let the prospect know that you'd love to set that up for them. You will be surprised how many people will set the appointment right then.

Leave a voicemail.

Don't just wait for your buyer to call. If you have a number, use it. If you don't get them on the phone, leave a message. Don't just hang up. This is a perfect opportunity to introduce yourself and tell them you are there to help in their home search.

Here's the hook. In your message, tell them that if they'd rather communicate via e-mail, you are going to send them an e-mail today for them to reply to. You are now asking them to return your e-mail, or to return your phone call. You give them the choice.

Call to confirm the appointment

Once you set an appointment, advise the prospect you will call to confirm the appointment. Establishing this up front shows the professionalism of the company and following through gives you the chance to make sure they are coming out.

Even though 90 percent of people search for a home online and the majority prefer to use e-mail to receive answers that doesn't mean you should never or will never get on the phone with people. Keep your phone skills fresh and continue to follow up.

Phone Scripts—Setting Appointments

Now that you have a customer on the phone, it's time to turn on the juice. This is where your product knowledge and access to information is invaluable. There is nothing better than an interested lead who you can help to find the perfect floorplan in the perfect community.

Most of the time, those calling only have one or two questions—usually, regarding price or availability. It is your job as an OSC to ask additional qualifying questions, encouraging them to open up and provide more critical information so you can further qualify them.

Once you learn more about their needs, you will be able to direct them to the perfect neighborhood. In most instances, you can reduce the options to a few (usually one) floor plans in a specific neighborhood. This is possible because you take the informative approach. As I mentioned before, providing an unbiased opinion towards any neighborhood will put customers at ease and build trust. When that trust is mutual, they will be more receptive to the advice you give and be ready to view the neighborhood or floorplan.

On the phone, you do not need to focus on selling/pushing a home; however, you can focus on setting the appointment by establishing urgency in many different ways. It is not your job to close the customer on a phone call, but it is your job to set the appointment. I compare the OSC's task of setting the appointment to the "closing" step in the traditional sales process.

Setting the appointment is essentially the "close" for the OSC. Just as the onsite sales agent must have several closing techniques ready to use, an OSC must have several "appointment setting" techniques and scripts to overcome objections for setting the appointment.

I have noticed that many OSCs do not ask for the appointment while talking to a lead on the phone. Instead, they answer the questions and dispense information. They hang up the phone feeling great, but have nothing to show for it.

Of course, not every lead is ready to visit your model home that day. When that is the case, do not hang up without asking for their contact information (e-mail address!!!!), so you can send a follow-up message, document, pictures, or sales flyers. Below are some great scripts that I have implemented. Once you get past the fear of asking, it actually becomes quite fun. Try it for one week and watch your number of appointments increase.

You have two goals for every phone contact:

- **Ask for the appointment.**
- **Obtain their full contact information, including e-mail address.**

The General Phone Conversation

Sales Counselor: Thank you for calling XYZ Homes. This is Mike.

Prospect: I have a question on this neighborhood, pricing, whatever ...

Sales Counselor: That's great. I am here to answer any questions you have. How may I help you today?

Answer questions and build urgency based on location, availability and rate of sale.

Sales Counselor: Have you had a chance to visit _____ neighborhood or view _____ home?

Prospect: No, I have not. (They might insert objection or condition here.)

Sales Counselor: I would love to arrange a time for you to visit _____ and see firsthand our model (or floorplan) and gather more information. How does this weekend/weekday look for you? (They might just say no. If so, continue to gather contact info.)

Sales Counselor: That's fine. What I can do is send you the information we have been speaking about (floorplan, details, community info, etc.). What is the best e-mail address to send this to?

What if some leads won't give you contact information? Don't sweat it. They are tire-kickers. Give them your phone number and make sure they know to visit your website for the latest information.

Overcoming Appointment Objections

Many times, customers will object to setting an appointment. Eventually, especially if they are somewhat interested, they will visit the community on their own. Take time to practice the following scripts and you'll be prepared to overcome some common objections.

Prospect: "We will just drive out when we have time and stop by the model. What are your hours?"

Sales Counselor: "Ms. Prospect, that is an option; however, we prefer to work by appointment. I have had many customers do the same thing and they ended up waiting around for the Sales Executive to finish working with a new home buyer or they do not even see the Sales Executive because s/he is out of the model home showing home sites to other customers.

Setting a time to visit that's convenient for you ensures that you receive the dedicated attention that you deserve. Now, that makes sense, doesn't it?"

Prospect: "I need to speak with my wife/husband/significant other before we come out."

Sales Counselor: "That's great, Ms. Prospect, and let me ask you this: If you did speak with wife/husband/significant other and they said whatever you thought was fine with them, would you prefer a weekday or the weekend?"

Prospect: "Weekend would be fine."

Sales Counselor: "Ms. Prospect, let's set up the appointment tentatively and you can check with your wife/husband/significant other and then call me back to confirm or change the time. Does that work for you?"

Prospect: "We're just looking right now."

Sales Counselor: "That's great. 'Just looking' is the fun part! I would love to be able to show you the quality and craftsmanship of our homes firsthand. By touring our model, you can review the details involved in owning a new home so that you can make future informed decisions—and we will be sure to keep in mind that you are 'just looking.'"

Prospect: "We have to sell our house first.

Sales Counselor: "That's no problem. In fact, most of our customers have to sell their homes in order to invest in a new home. But the first step is to determine which floorplan you might build and the time it will take to complete the home. I would love to set up a time for you to visit a model so you can gather all the information you need to make an informed decision. That makes sense, doesn't it?"

Prospect: "We aren't moving until next year."

Sales Counselor: "Next year will be here before you know it." In fact, our homes can take up to six months to complete from the ground up. Most home buyers like to know well in advance what their options are so they do not have to make a hurried decision. Can I set up a time to visit a neighborhood just so you can gather the information you need?"

Prospect: "We aren't moving for 2/3/5 years."

Sales Counselor: "That's fine. What I would like to do is to send you an occasional e-mail just to stay in touch. Then, when you are ready to look at our homes, you can contact me and I will help you determine the best neighborhood for your needs. How does that sound?"

Most people give you an objection because that is what they have been trained to do with salespeople. Once you have an arsenal of responses to these objections, they become less intimidating. Your job is to establish rapport and break down those barriers. After providing valuable information and building trust, the next logical step will be setting the appointment.

Get Rid of Model Home Hours!

When you give out the hours for your sales office and model home, you're giving away an opportunity.

Think about this. When a prospect calls and asks for your hours, what they're really saying is, "I'm interested and I'd like to come visit."

And what do you do? You tell them, "We're here from 10 to 6, Monday through Friday, and noon to 5 on weekends."

That's fine if you were a retail operation. But you're not selling $30 jeans or bagging up groceries in paper or plastic. You're a professional sales consultant working on an extremely important purchase, one of the biggest decisions an individual makes in a lifetime. Do you really want to leave it to chance that you're available when they happen to pop in? Can you risk losing this interested sales prospect to someone else?

Do you just walk into the office of your accountant, investment broker, or attorney when you feel like it? No, you make an appointment, because you want to be sure they are available when you arrive and that you have their undivided attention.

Why should new home sales be any different?

One of your primary sales goals is to set appointments with prospects. The next time someone calls for model hours, offer this dialogue instead:

"That is an option; however, we prefer to work by appointment to be sure you have someone available to answer your questions while you're here. We're happy to work around your schedule and set a time that's convenient for you."

Right away, you let this potential home buyer know that you care about their valuable time. You're not giving them a canned response, like "9 to 5, thanks and goodbye." If you just give the model hours, there's no interaction, no spark of a selling relationship, no effort. They got their answer and they will probably show up at some point—maybe while you're out grabbing lunch or running an errand. Or you might be tied up with another homebuyer. Regardless, you've missed a sales opportunity.

And one more thing...take your model home hours off your website. Don't make that face like I'm crazy. Instead, put a link that says, "For model home hours, click here or call." When they click, they see a screen that asks them to advise a convenient time so you can schedule an appointment. If they call, you slide into your script.

With just minor changes in the way you handle model home hour inquiries, you demonstrate that an appointment is in your home buyer's best interests. You'll discover your days become more productive because you're in control of your schedule and your leads.

Recording Your Phone Calls

It is amazing what happens when you record and listen to your phone calls. Once you get over the initial shock of how weird your own voice sounds, you can start to dissect the conversation and pinpoint ways to improve your delivery.

The first step, of course, is to take the time to record yourself talking with a customer. Ask others you trust to analyze it with you. Then, constantly improve your methods. Record every message you leave. You will hone your phone skills as you do this. Remember, most messages are relayed through non-verbal communication, such as facial expressions, posture, etc. When you speak on the phone, you are relying solely on your verbal communication. So, it is imperative that you are not focusing on what you should say next, but how you will say it. Memorizing your scripts will help you speak effectively on the phone.

In addition to memorizing and practicing your scripts, here are some excellent tips about better telephone communication:

- Maintain good posture.
- Smile when you talk—it comes through on the phone.
- Slow down your speech.
- Listen to the customer—do not interrupt.
- Ask multiple and engaging questions.
- Prepare in advance.

Leaving Powerful Voicemails

I've given you some examples of phone messages to utilize and personalize. One of the challenges you will face when leaving a message is how to craft the words that will produce actual results. Just leaving a message does not cut it. You need to have a prepared, professional presentation ready for every customer.

Voicemail gives you a 30-second spot in which you can promote your builder to someone who has expressed an interest in your homes. However, don't stop after just one message. The follow-up message can be equally as powerful and, when done right, will produce results. Just remember, there is a warm body on the other end of that phone line who is actually looking for a home.

Don't leave messages unprepared. Use the following tips to leave a professional voicemail that will get results:

✔ **Prepare for the message.** Review the lead and the details. Make reference to the contact source, questions, comments, or needs in your voicemail. Let the prospect know you are knowledgeable and prepared to assist them.

✔ **Choose the proper time to call.** The first call to an "A" lead should be right away if the lead came in during business hours. Double check to make sure they have indicated no objections to a phone call or requested a specific time to call. I have noticed that lunch hours are a good time to call with the follow-up. Never call in the evening unless it is requested. Only telemarketers call in the evening.

✔ **Leave a clear and concise message.** The message should be simple and cover the information that your customers requested when they submitted their inquiry. Quickly identify your reason for calling, talk about the area/home/homesite, and provide the prospect with your contact information. Let them know that you are available to serve them and it is in their best interest to return your call. Be sure to give them the next step. Let them know you will be following up by e-mail and ask for a return call. Finally, repeat your phone number twice and say it slowly so they have time to make a note.

Naturally, practicing these scripts does not guarantee a return call, but those customers who are truly interested will appreciate your promptness and professionalism. Also, this gives you plenty of chances to practice your delivery. So, take your game to the next level and record your voicemails to analyze how they sound. Make constant corrections and continually improve your delivery until it is second nature.

Pick up the Phone

When managing and following up with your leads, resist the temptation to hide behind e-mails to avoid rejection. Using e-mail properly is highly effective, but it is also the path of least resistance because the rejection is usually the lack of a return e-mail. You think "well, they must not be interested" and you continue to follow up on schedule without any response. This method is a very easy pill to swallow. But you need to take a step back and ask yourself, "Am I missing customers by not following up more frequently by phone?"

If a customer has provided their phone number, then you have another form of communication to get in touch with them. You have to think to yourself, "There is a buyer out there who is in the market." In addition, this is a "warm" lead, not a "cold" call, so the response from the customer is usually positive. There are a multitude of reasons why they did not respond to your e-mail or call you back from the initial message you left. They could be busy, forgetful, misplaced the e-mail, lost it to the SPAM boogie monster, or been on vacation. Depending on the level of interest, call them back a couple of times. Don't be timid. Make those few extra calls.

Be bold and don't worry about potential rejection. The ultimate goal of the follow-up process is to vet out true buyers and stop wasting your time on unqualified prospects.

Having said all that, you also shouldn't waste your time. There is no reason to follow up multiple times by phone with someone who has not responded to you after that first month. Hit them hard and fast in the first 30 days after the lead is submitted. This will help you determine true buyers. Then you can slide in a few calls over the long-term follow-up. Remember, the amount of leads is not the measure of success; only **appointments and contracts** will determine if you are spending your time following up with the right people.

The Phone/E-mail Combo: Like Peanut Butter and Jelly

Do you ever feel like some prospects never even existed? Are there times when you think that the initial request was submitted by a ghost?

As mentioned before, it is easy to hide behind e-mail and not make enough calls, but we have seen that when you blend these two together, like peanut butter and jelly, **magical things can happen**. Every time you send an e-mail can be a great excuse to pick up the phone and call—and vice versa. When you put these two tools together, you will notice that:

1. **Prospect response rates increase.**
2. **You reinforce your professionalism by providing both a verbal and written trail of your follow-up.**

Now, since neither of these mediums allows you to be face to face with your prospect, you must make sure that you focus on crafting the right message that will stand out from the crowd.

Just by following these simple steps, you will outpace other sales professionals who want your buyer.

Let's take a look at a sample e-mail/phone call double whammy:

Voicemail:

> Hi, Susan. My name is Mike with XYZ Homes. I received your request from our website for more information about a home.
>
> There certainly is a lot of information that you can get online, isn't there? I just wanted to let you know that I am here to provide fast answers to any questions you might have.
>
> I also have some specific information regarding your search that I would like to talk with you about.
>
> You can reach me at (insert phone number). Again that's (insert phone number). I will also send you a follow-up e-mail with my contact information.
>
> I look forward to discussing this information with you soon. Take care, Susan.

Now, right when you hang up, fire off an e-mail that goes something like this:

E-mail Subject Line: **Susan, Your Request from XYZ Homes**

Hello Susan,

My name is Mike Lyon with XYZ Homes. I just left you a brief voicemail and wanted to get in contact with you regarding your request for information on our website.

I know that searching for a new home can be overwhelming. I am here to help make that process easier. Not only can I provide fast answers to your questions, but I can also save you valuable time on your new home search.

I have some great information that I'd like to review with you. I look forward to hearing back from you soon. You can reach me at directly at (insert phone number).

I will be sure to follow up with you again by e-mail and phone in the next couple of days.

Thank you!

This establishes a few things in the buyer's mind:

1. **You are a professional.**
2. **You do what you say you will do. In your call, you say you will e-mail; in your e-mail, you say you will call.**
3. **You set the precedent that you are not going to give up.**
4. **You communicate that you are there to help.**

Now this is just an example of a first response. You can basically do this for every phase of the sales process. If your prospect has given you permission to follow up, then go for it! You never hear home buyers complain that "they just followed up too much". It is always the opposite: "Well I called/e-mailed and I never heard back."

You should not be timid in this area. In fact, in my experience of handling thousands of phone calls and thousands of e-mails, I can count on one hand the number of times I have had someone react negatively to me following up this way. Why do you think that is? Put yourself in the prospect's shoes. If they are a potential buyer who is actively looking, what do you think they will do? People are busy. There are numerous reasons why they don't respond right away, but eventually, you will invoke a response from active shoppers. They will gravitate towards the sales professional who follows up the best and provides the most relevant information.

You may not believe it, or maybe you think following up seven to ten times with a prospect in 30 days is too much. Well, I dare you to try it—if only for one month. **If it doesn't lead to more conversations, appointments, and sales, I'll let you slap me the next time we meet.**

The Best Time to Call

This is a common question from OSCs. I have always found that the afternoon will get you better results. [Side note: Calling real estate agents is fair game any time of the day.]

Over the past eight years. I've seen the following results:

- The time with the highest contact rate was between **2:00 and 6:00 PM.**
- Calls **made on Fridays** often have the best contact rates.

Of course, you should respond as soon as possible to any new lead. However, the times mentioned above would be good to keep in mind on the follow-up calls you make after you have left your first voicemail a day or two before. If you are having trouble connecting with a prospect at these specific times, make a note and try a different time on the next call.

Challenges and Solutions

I never want to stray too far from the sales prospecting trenches, so I recently decided to do a re-check of my phone skills. I picked up the phone and called a list of sales prospects. Yes, I was trying to convert them to appointments so I was putting my money where my mouth is!

Here are the results:

Total time spent: 182 minutes
68 prospects dialed
29 connected calls
24 voicemails left
15 bad/wrong numbers
66 minutes spent on voicemails and talking
61 minutes spent entering info/logging calls
55 minutes spent dialing

While I was making these sales prospect calls, I also monitored how I felt, what slowed me down, and other issues that contribute to productivity—or the lack thereof. I came up with some very interesting insights about myself that might impact you as well. Here is what I learned:

Challenge: *The best time to connect with a sales prospect (late afternoon) seems to be when I am the most tired.*

Solution: Crank through other tasks early in the morning. Create space in the afternoon for making these calls. Pace—don't push—yourself!

Challenge: *When I set the appointment, task switching derails me and slows down my momentum.*

Solution: Setting the appointment is one success. Ride this wave of positive action into the next call—and the next one and the next one. Use each appointment is one step on the ladder. You need more to get to the top! So take a note and tell the prospect you will send them the details after you are finished with your next call.

Challenge: *Interruptions cut into valuable phone time.*

Solution: Block out time for making calls and just say "No!" to distractions and interruptions—planned or unplanned. Stay focused so I don't lose my forward momentum.

Challenge: *Tasks presented by prospects divert me from making more calls.*

Solution: Make a note of what I need to do for follow-up so that I can tackle it after my phone time is completed. Communicate to the prospect when they will receive the information from me and be vigilant about meeting (or beating) that deadline.

Challenge: *The administrative task of logging sales calls, entering the leads into my database, and looking up information takes time.*

Solution: Stay organized and on point. Make brief notes while I'm on the roll of doing these calls and handle the administrative duties immediately after the blocked-out phone call period has ended. Don't chase the shiny objects. They'll only blind you!

7 Phrases to Help Set Appointments

Leads are great, but what value do they have unless you can convert the prospect into an appointment?

Remember, speed wins and in many cases, you not only need to be fast with your responses, but also fast to get them to meet in person. I believe every interaction with a lead, either on the phone or by e-mail, should have in mind the end goal of setting an appointment.

To do this, you need to be armed with some great "closing" scripts. In the lead management process, your first opportunity to "close" is setting the appointment. Here are seven phrases I have tested that work extremely well in this regard:

1. The Assumptive Close: "It seems like you are interested in this home. The next step would be to meet in person. What time would work for you?"
2. The Soft Close: "Thank you so much for taking the time to talk. What do you think about meeting in person for a VIP tour?"
3. The Trial Close: "Do you feel like you have enough information to take the next step and meet in person?"
4. The Hard Close: "What are we waiting for? Let's get together today!"
5. The "No Means Yes" Close: "You wouldn't mind if I asked you to set a time to meet in person, would you?"
6. The Tie Down Close: "I think an in-person meeting makes perfect sense, don't you?"
7. The Alternative Close: "I would love to set a time for a VIP showing. We have time during the week or on the weekend. Which works best for you?"

In most conversations, your prospect will give you all the chances you need to ask for the appointment. Remember, the appointment is merely the natural end to a great interaction. What is the worst they are going to say? "No." Go for the "No" every time. But don't give up. If they don't set the appointment right away be sure to have another reason to follow up with them and keep the conversation going.

CHAPTER SUMMARY

The phone is a powerful tool for the OSC. You must practice in order to perfect your delivery and increase your results. Be sure to use this tool frequently and take every opportunity to further qualify your lead. Don't fear calling the lead. Remember, there is an actual buyer on the other end of that phone.

Chapter Ten

LONG TERM
FOLLOW-UP

Using e-mail newsletters to stay in touch

The buying cycle for a new home can stretch out over many months. In fact, surveys often show us that many home buyers are still in the market six months later. Homebuilders' perceptions about the length of the research and buying cycle constitute about half of what consumers claim. For out-of-state and relocation buyers, this process can stretch out for more than a year. Although some buyers will purchase a home much quicker, this is usually a process that takes longer. So, don't give up communicating with a customer after your initial follow-up. I have witnessed many buyers schedule their first appointment one, two, three and even four years after their initial request from a website.

Once you have captured a lead, you need to make sure that you keep your builder's name in front of them. One of the most effective ways to do this is through ongoing e-mail marketing. This is not to be confused with your initial follow-up campaign for a lead. This is a general e-mail blast that can go out to all of your customers with the specific purpose of keeping your brand visible to them.

Some obvious benefits of e-mail marketing are:

- It helps build your brand and increase customer interaction.
- The return on investment is higher than in any other media (press, television, radio, direct marketing), according to the Direct Marketing Association's research.

- Tracking allows you to monitor the e-mail delivery results in real time and determine the number of recipients who opened the message and clicked on the links.
- It is fast. A study by Inverse Network Technology reveals that 91 percent of e-mail messages get to their final destination within five minutes.
- It is reliable. The above-mentioned study shows that in 95 percent of cases, the users have easy access to the e-mail message.
- It allows you to quickly and easily identify successful advertising methods and to change the message appropriately.

You have a growing database of leads—all of whom have requested information from you about buying or building a new home. It would be a travesty to not use this stockpile of customer information. In fact, more time should be spent cultivating your current database than in trying to attract new customers. These people are familiar with you and are in the market to purchase a new home. It is your job to spur them into action.

Well-crafted e-mail messages with powerful calls to action will gain results. You should expect to see at least the following averages from your e-mail campaigns:

- 20-30 percent Open Rate (the percentage of people who open the e-mail to read it)
- 9 percent Click-Through Rate (the percentage of people who opened the e-mail then clicked on a link)
- 1 percent Unsubscribe Rate (the amount of people who unsubscribe)

The Open and Click-Through Rate statistics I have seen have actually been higher, but the numbers above are a great benchmark. Highly targeted messages will see open rates approaching the 60 percent range.

You should, at minimum, send a general e-mail newsletter out to your customers at least once every month. I would be cautious about sending it more than once a month unless there is a special event or breaking news that a customer might like to know or you have a highly targeted message worth sharing. You do not want to discourage buyers from opening your newsletters by sending them too frequently. The goal is to stay in continual contact over a long period of time so that, when they do decide to buy, they will think of you first. That is not going to happen if you are over-communicating.

Lead Resuscitation: Revive your Prospects

If you have leads that have become lifeless and unresponsive, charge up the paddles and shock them back to life with what I call "lead resuscitation".

Many of you have a growing database of leads who have visited, called, or e-mailed you. This database should be the lifeblood of your sales efforts. What are you doing with it? Are you just looking for more prospects to file away or do you actively cultivate the possibilities that are tucked in there?

Don't just focus on the here and now. Avoid the temptation of the bright, shiny object that could detract from tending to this database that is chock full of potential sales. In other words, breathe new life into your stagnating leads.

There are three easy ways to resuscitate your dormant leads:

1. **Organize your database.** Keep your database up-to-date. Take one hour a week to clean up the list. Segment the leads into areas so that when you go to do your follow-up, you can easily focus on specific groups, like those who have either not responded at all or just not lately.

2. **Create an e-mail.** Develop a follow-up e-mail that you can personalize to your prospects. Using this format, you can follow-up more often with more leads. For example, take a chunk of leads that are six to nine months old and craft an e-mail marketing message. Make the e-mail appear as personal as possible—without getting too specific— and mail it to the group all at once. Now you've maximized your time and potentially revived some dying leads.

3. **Pick up the phone.** Yes, go old school. Make personal contact with those people you just e-mailed. Combining the one-two punch of e-mail and phone follow-up is like charging up those defibrillator paddles and zapping those leads with your sales pizzazz.

You might be surprised by how many of those prospects are still in the market. You'll probably also encounter many who have had a change in their situation and, because you're the only one following up, you hit them at the perfect time to convert the lead into a sale!

Don't let your valuable leads die. Shock them back into the home-buying mode. I promise, it won't hurt a bit.

Crafting the Message

Half the battle of creating powerful e-mail campaigns is developing great content to send to your customers. Here are examples of reasons to follow up with your customers that you can include in your e-mail campaigns:

1. Highlight the Online Sales Counselor and the benefit of the services s/he provides
2. Provide updates on financing and interest rates
3. Announce new and coming-soon communities
4. Extend any special offers or incentives
5. Highlight builder's achievements or awards
6. Introduce new floor plans
7. Announce the opening of additional phases

8. Highlight the benefits of owning a new home versus a resale home

9. Explain your building process

10. Share a satisfied customer's story

11. Feature your services and warranties

12. Highlight community or neighborhood events

13. Review the strong points of your website

14. Offer news and statistics about general homebuilding and new construction

15. Send holiday greetings

All of these can be set up as educational or informative articles that subtly lead the buyer back to the blog on your website. You can even include industry articles from other sources (with permission), thereby limiting the time you spend developing new material. Crafting your campaigns to look like news instead of a sales pitch will build trust.

In addition to the articles, you will always need to include the following in an obvious, but understated way:

- Easy "Contact Us" button and text throughout
- Latest promotion for your builder—people love a deal
- Move-in ready homes or new communities
- Quick links to the website
- Link to financing options

The message can change frequently, but it is recommended that you keep a similar look and feel to brand the newsletter and your company.

Segmenting Your List

Segmenting your list is the process of dividing your e-mail list into subgroups, based on what your subscribers have in common. Here are example groups that can be used to segment your database of leads:

- General lead
- Area or community of interest
- Customer has responded
- Customer has visited a community
- Customer is on contract
- Customer has closed on the home
- Realtor

Targeting e-mail campaigns to each of these individual segments will increase the likelihood of a response to your message or offer. For homebuilders, segmenting your list and targeting the communication efforts pay off in higher open and click-through rates—which will ultimately lead to increased sales.

One-to-one communication is especially important for homebuilders since new home shoppers have more information at their fingertips. You can increase these "personal" messages by creating a targeted, more meaningful connection with customers through the segmentation of your leads database.

Don't make the mistake of measuring success from your e-mail campaigns by the number of e-mails sent. You need to measure the results—the number of "opens" and clicks on calls-to-action. One way to ensure that your customers will open your campaigns is to make your messages personal and relevant. A buyer who is on contract and well into the building process will not want to hear about a new promotion in the neighborhood where they just purchased a home. Similarly, a customer who has not even responded does not want to participate in an "after the sale" survey.

Take time to go through your list and segment it properly. This will require a time commitment up front, but will deliver great results in the end. Also, once you have defined your interest categories, you can make the proper adjustments going forward.

E-mail Marketing Tools

If your CRM does not have the capability to send e-mails that track open rates or allow for the user to unsubscribe, then you need to use one of the many web-based e-mail marketing systems that are available for your monthly e-mail blasts.

Most systems have the ability to:

Easily create powerful e-mail campaigns

- Choose from customizable HTML e-mail templates
- No technical skills necessary
- Advanced features for professionals

Build and manage your e-mail lists

- Easily import existing e-mail addresses or lists
- Customized visitor sign-up for your website
- Powerful e-mail list-management features

Track e-mail campaign results

- How many e-mails were delivered and opened
- Names of contacts who opened each e-mail and clicked through
- The links that generate the most clicks
- Allows user to unsubscribe with ease

Get your e-mails delivered

- Automatic formatting ensures your e-mails look professional wherever they arrive!
- ISP (internet service provider) relationships optimize e-mail delivery and keep you off of the SPAM lists
- Full SPAM compliance

Why Do We Need E-mail Marketing When We Have Social Media?

Social media has added a new and powerful marketing tool to the marketing arsenal. But many people are squeezing social media so hard that they have forgotten about the "old-fashioned" e-mail marketing campaign. In fact, this is a comment I frequently hear: "With all of these status updates, tweets, article postings, video sharing, and more, we just don't need the e-mail campaigns like we used to."

When I speak to homebuilders about using social media to generate new home sales, I always start with this thought:

"Even though we are here to talk about social media and how you can leverage that network, the bottom line is, home buyers are not going out to search for a home on Facebook. You must have a solid foundation and a bullet-proof online sales program, before you invest all of your time and effort building a social media campaign."

One of the key internet marketing tools in your Online Sales Program is your e-mail marketing. If you aren't sending out monthly campaigns to potential customers, realtors, and past customers, then you are missing valuable opportunities.

"But we have 1,000 followers on Twitter and 400 Facebook fans. They all see our stuff."

Great—now, does your post stick around indefinitely? No, it's short-lived—which is why e-mail campaigns are so great.

Let's look at some of the benefits of this form of marketing:

- **E-mail campaigns are targeted.** Unlike a tweet, you can guarantee that e-mail recipients almost always see the subject line. Your challenge is to make that subject line engaging enough for the recipient to want to open your e-mail.
- **E-mail campaigns are more permanent.** When the e-mail is in someone's inbox, they have to delete it to get rid of it. A Facebook status update or an article will disappear on its own, as newer ones displace it. So, an e-mail "lives" until the recipient takes action.
- **E-mail campaigns have more real estate.** E-mails offer more space to talk about your message link to other information, and add enticing images, which is much more powerful than the 140 characters allowed by Twitter.
- **You can track the effectiveness of e-mail campaigns.** Tracking an e-mail's effectiveness is easier and less time-consuming than tracking the ROI of social media.
- **You can take action with e-mail campaigns.** With a targeted e-mail message, you can actually see who opens and clicks through to the specific link. When you drill down into that data, you can then pick up the phone, call the prospect or realtor and talk about the subject immediately. Very powerful stuff!

If you really want to kick it old school, look at direct mail. When executed correctly, it can still be very effective. Like a diverse portfolio, you must always keep your marketing program well-rounded. Just because there is a great new technology or a new advertising medium, it doesn't mean the old method is useless (unless it is a newspaper!). You always have to look at the return on time and investment to determine its value for you or your company.

CHAPTER SUMMARY

We all know one-to-one communication is the most effective form of marketing. This is the true nature of the onsite sales agent. Conducting this form of marketing was expensive in the past. However, new technology has made it affordable. You can deliver a message to 1 or 1,000 for the same investment of money and time.

Through targeting and customer segmentation, you can personalize the message and guarantee a higher response. Start small and grow with time. The return on investment will be tremendous when you utilize this valuable tool.

Chapter Eleven

SOCIAL MEDIA
FOR HOME BUILDERS

How to build powerful online communities

I want to be clear on this. There is a right way and a wrong way to execute a social media strategy, especially in our business. Many builders are stuck on trying to apply the wrong marketing methods to a new medium. I don't want to use this chapter as a "how-to" or to explore the individual social networking sites. I would rather talk about the concepts that are universal when applied to this form of communication.

Yes, that is right, I said "communication". We can't just think of Facebook as a marketing avenue to push our message out. Twitter shouldn't be a one-way street where you talk but don't listen. We should be encouraging connection and communication. We should be in the content creation business, sharing ideas and information to the world and soliciting feedback.

I really don't think the platform matters as much as we think; platforms will come and go. A recent survey revealed that more than half of Americans thought Facebook was a passing fad.

Fad or not, and regardless of the medium, we know that **great content, easily shared, on the platforms that we all use will always get you the results you want!**

But that is often not what your social media program looks like. Take a moment to analyze your own social media marketing program. If you are like many of the builders who talk to me, your strategy may be similar to this:

- We have a blog, but we barely post any new content—and when we do, it's not so great.
- Our Facebook fan page got off to a great start, because we really pushed it, but our engagement is down and I'm worried that customers are going to post bad things on it—or stop coming.
- On Twitter, we just link our posts from Facebook—not much going on there.
- Now we're on to Pinterest (or fill in the next shiny new social network here) because everyone is talking about it. Geez, I can't keep up.
- Oh, by the way, we don't encourage our sales people to use Facebook—it's a productivity killer.
- Google +...should I really sign up for that?

Ok, I'm going to the extreme here but I bet these problems and concerns resonate with many of you. Because I work with so many builders, and I'm a big believer in the power of these tools, I constantly ask myself, "Why?" Why is it such a struggle for my clients? Why is it such a struggle for our industry? Why aren't customers more willing to engage?

If you ask yourself "Why?" often enough, the answers will become evident. We struggle because we are going after the wrong things in the wrong way. Enough about why it isn't working. Let's talk about how to get a solid program rolling.

The formula for a homebuilder does not have to be complicated. The first step to building a more engaged audience is to pursue the right people. Who are our "right people"? I suggest that we should actively reach out to the real estate agent community and our current customers. These are people who already care about us and what we have to say. They are also people who would spread a message with very little prodding. Think about a new prospect walking in the door. What is their motivation to "like" our Facebook page or follow us on Twitter? Until they're invested in us, there is little chance. On top of that, what is the likelihood they are going to communicate anything on our behalf. Now, I'm not saying we don't engage these people (in fact, I'll share a great method to increase engagement from prospects in just a moment). It's just that we sometimes spend too much time chasing the wrong people.

Now think about a real estate agent. Many of them are professionals, reading books on social media (hopefully my book, "Social Media Guide for Real Estate") going to seminars, reading blogs, and watching webinars. They are happy…no…ecstatic to connect, engage, build their connections and have conversations. In fact, the things you share could have a direct impact on them. So go after them with a vengeance.

What about your current and past customers? Assuming they are invested in you and love your product, you should do everything within your power to encourage them to share their experience, photos, feedback, and anything about the process with their network. Many of them already are; we just don't know because we aren't connected. Encourage them to "check in" at their new community, post pictures of the building process, participate in contests, etc. In fact, the million-dollar idea is actually rewarding them for these activities. This is what is called "gaming theory". A simple example of this in other industries, "check in" and get a coupon for your coffee. Look at LinkedIn. When you sign up, you will notice your status is only 80 percent complete until you enter in your school info and have one recommendation. This motivates someone to participate and complete activities so they get a reward or complete the tasks. Younger generations are hard-wired for this because we've been playing Super Mario Brothers our entire life, completing level after level and not feeling complete until we rescue the princess from King Koopa.

But if we are going to inspire them to share our information, we need to train our staff on how to educate their prospects to use it—and have a trackable program in place to check the progress. If your sales team doesn't know how to use these networks or isn't engaged with them, there is a good chance your prospects and customers won't be either. It's a two-way communication channel, so be sure that your team is actively using their social networks. Again, it doesn't have to be complicated and once everyone understands, the social effect will be tremendous.

The Check-in Challenge

Of course, you should leverage anyone who walks in your door. But the question is, what is the motivation for anyone to "like" your page? Well, if they are an interested prospect, they should want to connect just because you asked. But even if they aren't, we can easily incentivize them on the spot to "check-in" and "like" our page. I will use Facebook as the example because most people have an account and will know what to do (of course, this can work with other platforms like FourSquare, but only a few of your customers will be active).

- Set up your place on Facebook (Google this if you need to figure out how).
- Get some cheap gift cards; I like the customized $5 Starbucks gift cards with your logo on it.
- Create a promotional banner that shows your prospect or customer what they will get when they check-in.
- Encourage your sales reps to ask all prospects to check-in.
- Enter them in a giveaway to win an additional contest if they snap a photo and include that with their check-in, too.
- Have the prospect show you their check-in and give them a gift card

It's that easy. What would the cost be? Well, let's do the math.

- 100 new prospects a month
- 65% will check-in or access their Facebook account
- 65 gift cards at $5 each = $325
- Average friends on Facebook =130
- Network reach = 8,450 every month
- TOTAL COST: $.04 per eyeball who sees their friends check-in

I don't know about you, but I like those numbers. This is word-of-mouth marketing on steroids. These check-ins are going to reach their peer group—people who are most likely in the same market and same demographic that actually care about what they are doing.

The same concept can work with your digital visitors those people who visit your website and are interested in your products. But you have to give them a reason to "like" you; whether it is a promotion or event, drive that action.

Empower Frontline Employees

It seems that builders are reluctant to release some of the control to their local agents. Understandably, they are concerned about controlling the message. I have often presented the idea of creating a community blog, Active Rain account, or a community-specific e-mail campaign. Then I follow that up with the recommendation that the salesperson create the content, and the response usually goes like this:

"Whoa, who, what, hang on....We don't want our salespeople writing for us...They're not the best writers...I'm worried about:

- What they will say
- The kind of pictures they will use
- Will they get permission to use the photos?
- What if the person gets fired?

- What if this person is a disgruntled employee who we may want to let go…That might be better running through corporate…We have to keep the brand consistent…ad nauseum.

By trying to control the message too much, builders miss potential connections with very good customers who are craving transparency.

[Side note: Your sales execs are already sending out hundreds of e-mails and communicating with customers every day. Are you controlling that message?]

These new home buyers don't want the story from "corporate". They want it from the guy on your team—probably the sales executive—who actually knows the families who just moved into the neighborhood, why they moved, what their concerns were, how the schools are, whether the neighborhood is safe, and so on.

They don't want to see stock photography of kids at the park. They want photographs of actual families unloading their moving truck and eating pizza—sweat, bad hair, and all!

A customer nowadays will typically prefer to see rough video shot on an iPhone and uploaded to YouTube, because it is real, not "produced".

I'm not saying there isn't a place for a more polished product. In fact, that usually needs to happen first to build credibility and attract the customer. But after you attract, how do you engage—**I mean, really engage**—online?

No longer do we control the whole message. The internet has shifted the power to the consumer. As many of the larger builders have realized, it doesn't take long for user-generated "bad press" to get out there.

The building industry must step it up. Sales agents must create their own user-generated "good press". Tell the positive stories about your communities. Take the sales presentation to the web. Engage locally with your prospects, and with your Realtors!

Real estate is becoming hyper-local. The great Realtors are creating a local presence and becoming the experts in their niches. And they are seeing the results! Shouldn't a new home sales agent have the same opportunity?

The old saying goes: "Better to ask for forgiveness than for permission." **Exercise your ninja skills and create something outside of "corporate".**

Don't Be Boring

There has been a recurring question/statement lately regarding social media status updates and the relevance of Twitter. It usually goes like this "Ok, so I understand Facebook and friends and all that stuff, but seriously, what's up with Twitter? Who cares what you had for breakfast? I don't get it."

My response is this: If that's your take on it, you are following boring people. People who are boring offline will most likely be boring online. It is always the goal to not be boring, trivial, mundane, commonplace, or self-absorbed with your messages.

The follow-up question to this statement is usually, "OK, so then what am I supposed to post on Twitter that is not boring or 'salesy'? I have a message that I want to get out there but don't want to be that guy."

That is the question of the day. In fact, I struggle with it as well. So I always strive to write something that will get a response, comments, shared, or retweeted.

You are in real estate. You want people to know that you sell homes. You want to update your Facebook status or send out a tweet to tell the world.

Here is the lazy way: **"Are you thinking about buying a home? I have three great homes ready right now."**

With this phrasing, the shields go up and everyone who sees the update shifts into defense mode. No one likes to be sold, especially not in their social network safe zone.

Now here is a creative way to say the same thing: **"Another happy family just moved in to The Oaks—this community is filling up with great people. I love it!"**

Some choose to wish people good morning and tell them goodnight via Twitter. Some people update their status and describe the sandwich they are eating for lunch or what they are cooking for dinner. Some people tell others why it is so good to do business with them or their company.

No matter what you decide to post, run it through the "Does anyone care what I am saying" filter. Ask yourself these questions:

- Is this trivial? If I said this to someone in real life, would they look at me funny? If it is trivial, is it at least funny (I guess it would have a humor value then)?
- Does this matter to my network of people (whether it is personal or professional)?
- Will this be retweeted? Is the content cool enough to be spread?
- Is this negative? Should I even be saying it?
- Will this encourage someone or add value to my network?
- If my message has to do with a meal I am eating, is that because I am a professional chef, cooking is a passion for me, or there is some

lesson others can learn from my food choice—e.g., "3rd time I was food poisoned by Eggroll Kingdom—stay away"?

If you have to justify what you are saying, you probably should nix it or find a more creative way to say it. Again, I am basing this on the goal of enriching and increasing your professional life. **There is nothing wrong with posting updates with no significance on Twitter or Facebook if you don't expect an outcome or results.** This is just advice if you actually want an audience to notice you—in a good way, not the high school drama queen way.

Keep in mind that your digital personality is an extension of your actual personality. Just as boring people are boring offline and online, so are talkative people, mean people, sarcastic people, "debbie-downers", etc.

All these new digital tools are just a method of connection and communication. Those who take the time to develop valuable content and give more back to their network will always be noticed, followed, friended, retweeted, and shared.

Now, I personally post a lot of stuff that never gets retweeted, but I do try to take my own medicine and always aim to give value and entertain.

Swimming in the Social Stream

Something unique about social media is the flow of information in real time, whether it's tweets or status updates on Facebook or LinkedIn. You might even say it is more like a "fire hose" of information than a stream. It can be tough to keep up with all this information, like trying to get a drink from a fire hose.

What is interesting is the difference between "traditional" Web and Web 2.0. The traditional Web is more permanent. Web 2.0 is transient, or as I heard it described to me once, "New media is like a paper cup. You use it and then throw it away."

For example, if you miss a tweet on Twitter, it soon fades away. As newer tweets pop up, the others get pushed farther down in the stream and eventually off to the next page. Or the post is pushed out past your 100 updates on Tweetdeck. Gone.

Such fleeting moments are the social aspect of Web 2.0. It's like walking into a party. You don't walk around to everyone and ask, "What did I miss?" On Facebook, the same holds true. You're not going to go back every 15 days to see what you've missed on every single person. You may go back and look at the interesting people, but you're really only interested in what's happening in the here and now. Anything older than a few days is ancient history. The same holds true for Twitter. What is happening today? Are you showing up in the "here and now"? You should spread out your posts so you're not posting too frequently. Post insightful information and ideas that prompt other people to talk about it and comment back. This is the foundation of internet marketing and PR at its finest.

So, what gets the conversation going in "Real Estate 2.0"?

1. **Create interesting, informative content.** Piquing interest is the easiest way to increase exposure.
2. **Stay relevant and noteworthy.** While some readers might find it fun to hear about your pet's last trip to the litter box, avoid the temptation. Stay relevant and focus on your audience.
3. **Time your updates.** Just as there is a good time to send an e-mail for maximum visibility, there is also a best time to update your status or send a tweet. Saturday at midnight is not good because your readers aren't online. What day and time will your audience be looking? Send your information then.

4. **Engage others.** You will get more "action" when you hold real conversations online. More people will talk about and promote you if you are practicing this twist on the golden rule: "Listen to others as you would want them to listen to you."

5. **Put the conversation first.** If your only social media goals are marketing, traffic, and exposure, you've missed the whole point of this medium. This is Real Estate 2.0 and it starts with the conversation. Chat now. Sell later.

Does Your Social Media Content Suck?

With plenty of builders jumping into social media, the questions I have been getting a lot are, "What now?" and "What kind of content should we be posting and where do we come up with the content?"

So you have your Twitter account with hundreds of followers, your Facebook page with fans, and a blog ready for posting. That's all good, but now you have to come up with content.

Social media/networking/marketing—whatever you want to call it—is a two-way conversation. It is a dialogue, not a monologue. So if you are trying to take the same methods used in other marketing sources and cram them into the social media box, you might as well quit while you're ahead.

It's not all about you. We know you build homes. We know you have homes for sale. We know you are the best. Tell the audience something of value that they might want to pass along. I will venture to say that your audience doesn't care as much about the "home of the day" as you do. Again, if the higher ups look at your efforts and say, "We need to talk more about us," they may not be educated on social media and you need to school them!

This is a whole new ballgame. The rules are completely different. This is why it has presented a tough challenge for builders.

Ultimately, your goal is to connect with the right people and establish yourself as the thought leader in a specific area. Ask yourself what those areas are and this is where your content will come from. For example:

Real Estate. You are a builder, watching the numbers, market data, permits, and sales. Post content about that. What is happening in the local real estate market that is interesting? What would realtors like to know about? Create content related to those topics.

Local Economy. The housing industry is heavily dependent on jobs and the local economy. Report on good news that affects your town or county. Highlight the uniqueness of your city and the development that is occurring, like new or expanding businesses. Present a preview of what is going to be developing next in your town.

Green Building. Eco-friendly homes are hot right now. A large majority of builders are either ENERGY STAR-certified or use a lot of ENERGY STAR products. Heck, you might even be LEED certified. Position yourself as the authoritative figure on green building. Show people the difference and how much they can save by going green. Talk about new products and get people excited to be part of this trend.

First-time Buyers. These newbies compose a high percentage of today's buyers, and they need to be educated on the process. Show them why they need to "fire their landlord" and start paying themselves. Keep in mind that they are also the most active on the social media platforms.

Financing. Right now, financing is a HUGE issue and one of the best closing tools. Share financing data and statistics on the national and local level. Become the financing expert and break the data down so the average buyer can understand. People need to know that now is the time to buy!

Local Events. Share local events and happenings occurring around the area to showcase your community as an active place to live. Everyone wants to be in on the fun, so share that with the world. I recently wrote a blog post for a builder about the local Home & Garden Show and it pulled in the most hits and traffic on his site.

School District. As you well know, one of the largest factors in the location and choice of a new home and community is the school district. Share info about the schools like reports, events, and issues that the parents will appreciate knowing.

Feature Your Employees. This is a fantastic way to promote your people without selling. Talk about their activities, recent achievements, and interests. The social aspect of this new media gives the customer a chance to get to know you better.

Talk About Yourself. Yes, it is actually ok to talk about yourself, but do it right. Share the things that are newsworthy—awards, community openings, events, sponsorships, and mentions in the news. Just don't tell your audience over and over that you are a builder and they need to buy a house.

These are just a few ideas to get you started on finding the right content for these platforms. Remember, you also need to engage. Comment on other blogs, retweet good info, and take part in a conversation. Ultimately, it is about connecting with others.

Don't "Waste" Your Time on Social Networking

"How in the world am I supposed to keep up with all of this social media stuff? I don't have enough time as it is!"

The last thing you want social networking to be is a time sucker, especially if it replaces critical business development opportunities. My advice is don't spend more than 45 minutes a day of your "business" time on social networking.

I have yet to see someone be 100 percent efficient from 8 to 5 every single day. So allocate some of that wasted time to your digital network. On that same note, don't get caught in what we call "digital quicksand" where you emerge hours later and realize you have been doing nothing but playing Mafia Wars.

It may look like I spend more time on these sources than others, but I follow my own advice. I have a few tools that allow me to be efficient. (tweetdeck, hootsuite, buffer, to name a few) but my Swiss Army knife is my iPhone, loaded with all of my social networking apps. Because I am connected, **I can maximize my "down time" for connecting with others—yet another reason** to trade in your dumb phone for a smartphone.

Think of all the times when you are waiting around—like getting your oil changed, waiting for the dentist, waiting around the mall for your wife or kids to finish shopping. This is a great time to pop onto Facebook and talk to a few folks, tweet or retweet, or comment on a LinkedIn discussion.

If you are committed to using social networking to build your business, this is how you can do it without wasting time. Or you can just stop watching the latest reality show that is so-awesome-seriously-you-have-to-watch-it-cause-it's-soooooo-good and use that time to build your brand. **Some call that being a workaholic; I just call it smart business.**

Cracking the Facebook Algorithm, Edgerank

Does it feel like you are talking to the clouds on Facebook? Are you frustrated with the lack of response you are getting from your Facebook page?

If you are using your Facebook profile or business page to build influence and awareness, then you must make sure people actually see you. Getting the visibility you seek on Facebook can be a challenging, and for some, a daunting task. With over 800 million users, the Facebook community is a little crowded, and with crowds comes noise, and noise makes it harder to capture the attention of your audience.

In order to address the cluttered stream (or fire hose for some), Facebook organizes your news feed by an algorithm that works to determine what will be the most important posts for you to see.

Many users ask me, "So what does it take to make it into this party called the 'top news'?"

Well, Facebook has an algorithm for that, and unlike Google, it's not a secret. In fact, at a recent developer's conference , they laid it all out in a formula. Facebook refers to the algorithm as "EdgeRank".

So let's break this down. Facebook is relying on three main properties to determine if it will show your post in users top news feed.

1. **Affinity**
2. **Weight**
3. **Recency**

What do these three factors actually mean?

Affinity Score: The number Facebook assigns, based on the actual connection between the content creator and the user.

For example, if you frequently check in on a connection or page, they will make that connection between the two and display the content those people or pages post more frequently in your feed.

Weight Score: Every post, share, or update receives a score based on the number of comments or likes it receives. This factor reinforces the need for interaction. A post with no comments or likes will have an extremely low chance of appearing in the top news feed and will float down the stream unnoticed.

Recency Score: This refers to when the content was shared. Facebook gives another preference to recent content and will push down the older posts. Yes, older posts will show up, but rarely if older than 48 hours—and they have to be from a good connection and with a lot of comments and likes.

So the perfect update, either from your page or personal profile, needs to be recent, appeal to your friends and connections and receive a lot of comments and likes. Congratulations! You just cracked the code to the top news feed.

The reason that Facebook shares this—as opposed to Google keeping the algorithm a heavily guarded secret—is because the site relies on other people to participate to make the system work effectively.

You can't force people to comment or like, but you can encourage. You can't make bad content look good, and you can't fake affinity or a friendship.

So you now you know what EdgeRank is, the next question is, "How can I make this work for me?"

Here is the secret formula:

1. **Content Is King:** Create and share really good content (informative, funny, enlightening, timely, insightful).

2. **Listen More:** By spending more time commenting and talking to others, you build powerful relationships.

When you pay attention to others, they will pay attention to you. If you post content they like, then you will get the awareness you are looking for. So it all boils down to a little bit of hard work.

Whoever Said This Was Easy Was Lying!

Are you finding yourself discouraged with your attempt at building your online brand? Some people become frustrated and abandon ship altogether or even worse, have left their blogs looking like a digital ghost town. I hope you did not buy into those touting that this would be "easy". Nothing that has value is ever easy. Yes, it is easy to sign up for a Facebook account, create a Twitter account, and shoot a YouTube video. Yes, it is easier than ever before to reach a target audience. But creating quality content and building influence requires something else entirely: passion and dedication. Just to make sure you are covering all the bases, here are 19 steps to ensure you make it past the three-month "flake out" mark that has been claiming many victims.

1. Determine your unique areas of expertise and passion.
2. Create a clear vision. Develop a concise positioning statement. (e.g.,"Your one-stop for Austin real estate news")
3. Buy a domain name that people can remember.
4. Make a list of at least 52 weeks of blog ideas, one for each week of the year.

5. Pick the medium that makes sense for you: articles, video, audio, or a combination.

6. Set up your blog (I highly recommend WordPress) and install a great theme or work with a web designer to set it up for you (money well spent).

7. Add the appropriate plug-ins to help you manage your new blog, like scheduling your posts in advance to upload at specific days and times.

8. Make sure that people can easily share your content; use the Facebook "like", tweetmeme, and other sharing features.

9. Create a Facebook fan page and polish up your Facebook personal profile.

10. Create your LinkedIn profile and add all the relevant info.

11. Set up your YouTube account.

12. Start posting all your new content.

13. Connect all of your sources together and distribute your message.

14. Generate awareness by reading and commenting on other similar blogs. Be sure to encourage comments and respond on your own blog.

15. Create your Twitter account, spend time finding those in your target market, industry or area of passion, and follow them.

16. Join as many active Facebook fan pages and groups relating to your blog topic as possible.

17. Make sure you promote your blog/site on all relevant materials, especially your e-mail signature.

18. Request guest posts and comments from other professionals in your industry.

19. Don't forget to create and cultivate a robust e-mail database using MailChimp or Constant Contact

Yes, 19 items seems like a lot of work—because it is. Many people have mistakenly thought that building a personal brand online is easy with all of these new tools at our fingertips. What we have seen happen is now that EVERYONE is online, it is critical to develop solid content and spend the time building a community that will **listen to you.**

So if you are serious, print this out, post it by your desk and execute... every single day.

CHAPTER SUMMARY

I'm confident that many things have already changed since this edition was published, so I hope you are making the effort to constantly learn and change with your market and consumer preferences.

Remember: Don't get caught in digital quicksand. Create a strategy around your goals and execute on that strategy every day.

Chapter Twelve

PRE-SALE
CAMPAIGN

Attracting buyers before the community opens

One of the highest conversion actions on a builder's website is the "Coming Soon" registration. Whether your market is "hot" or not, a pre-sale campaign will capture many leads who are eager for more news about your upcoming neighborhoods. The pre-sale process is fairly simple and one that every builder should consider. When you use online marketing to do the work for you, a pre-sale campaign can be inexpensive and effective.

The general components of a pre-sale campaign are:

- Feature the "Coming Soon" community on the website.
- Post a "Coming Soon" sign at the community entrance.
- Implement direct mail advertising to target zip codes to bolster interest.
- Establish a priority registration database.

With a minimum marketing investment, you can start building your priority list. Most of your traffic and registrations will come from your website and the directional sign near your community. You should already be spending a good amount of money driving traffic to your website. Now you can start building your priority registration list from the traffic you receive.

The Pre-sale Process

The follow-up process will vary, based on the customer's interest, the builder, community, and time period before the grand opening.

In most cases, you can use all or part of this process to create a buzz and keep potential buyers out of the market in anticipation of your new community. You should drive all registrations through your website to funnel into your lead management system. The priority registration form should have the following fields—and all should be required.

First Name
Last Name
E-mail Address
Phone Number
Street Address
City
State
Zip Code

How did you hear about our new community? (drop down of choices)

It's not necessary to add a "Comments" section. Most customers will ask you the same questions: "When will it open?" and "How much are the homes?"

You can address these questions up front on your Priority Program FAQ's. Here are examples of the important questions you can answer:

- **What is the Priority List?**

Explain how the program works and the benefits of registering.

- **Why is there a Priority List for this community?**

Explain the need to make the first selections of the homes and homesites fair, because this new neighborhood is in high demand. Also, let them know that people on the Priority List will be able to purchase first and at the best price.

- **Why should I join the Priority List?**

Advise them that they will be contacted in advance with up-to-date information on the progress of the community and the grand opening event. This insider information is only for those on the Priority List.

- **How do I join the Priority list?**

Explain that joining is simple, and their contact information is confidential.

- **If I join the list, am I under any obligation to buy a home?**

Assure them that this is only a list to keep them informed of the progress, not a contract.

- **What happens after I join the Priority list?**

Explain that you will be contacting them via e-mail as the community progresses. Also, when the grand opening is planned, they will receive details on the groundbreaking event.

After the customer registers, you should start the follow-up process. Here is a great snippet from an e-book by Kevin Oakley, *"Pre-sale Without Fail"*. Kevin is a branding and marketing expert specializing in the new home industry. He is the Director of Marketing & Sales Training at Heartland Homes, a top 100 national builder (and Pittsburgh's #1 custom home builder). **He believes results matter, brands are not dead, and that it's not easy—but it IS simple.** Learn more at www.brandpossible.com.

This is the timeline that he has used multiple times with great success. You can download the e-book for free at www.presalewithoutfail.com.

Let's take a look at an overview of the Pre-Sale Without Fail program from start to finish, and then we will take a look at each step in more detail.

90 Days Prior to Preview Event
(or as early as possible if you are not worried about cannibalizing current offerings)

- Install marketing sign and put community on your website (no pricing!).

60 Days Prior to Preview Event

- Send direct mail to area zip codes: "Coming Soon" postcard #1.

50 Days Prior to Preview Event

- Send direct mail to area zip codes: "Coming Soon" postcard #2.

45 Days Prior to Preview Event

- Send press release to local media.
- Update blog.
- Place a small ad in LOCAL newspaper (optional) to announce the event.

30 Days Prior to Preview Event

- Enter the pricing in your internal system for houses only (not homesite premiums).
- Begin scheduling appointments to narrow house selection.
- Add base house prices to your website.

20 Days Prior to Preview Event

- Send event invitations to your database: "You're Invited to a VIP Event" (fold-over invitation)

15 Days Prior to Preview Event

- Do follow-up phone calls and emails to database.

2 Days Prior to Preview Event

- Send reminder emails and make phone calls to RSVP list.
- Send a video email to those who haven't responded.
- Mark-up site map and grading map with premiums and features for each home site.

Presale Without Fail PREVIEW EVENT

- Reveal grading/plat maps, timelines for development/construction to begin.
- Goal at the event is to set up appointments with new prospects, and schedule appointments to finalize home site selection with those who have already narrowed down house type.

1 Day After Preview Event

- Publish blog posts showing activity at the event.
- Announce "Grand Opening" publicly on your website.
- Begin appointments to finalize paperwork/hold appointments with new prospects.

2 Days After Preview Event

- Send direct mail to database and zip codes: "Plat Map" postcard.
- Email "Plat Map" to databases.

GRAND RELEASE EVENT

- Completed contracts with hand money accepted on first come, first served basis.

2 Days After Grand Release

- Send press release sent to local media.
- Update blog.

1-2 Weeks After Grand Release

- Send press release sent to local media.
- Update blog.
- Send direct mail and email to database and zip codes: "We Sold X Number of Homes".

The demand for the community and the amount of time until it opens will determine how many and at what frequency you will send your e-mails. E-mail is the easiest and most cost effective form of direct marketing and it allows you to stay in constant contact. Tailor an interesting message well before you know the specific details of your new community.

Some ideas you can use to keep the buyer interested are:

- Area details
- City information
- Neighborhood amenities
- Floor plan amenities
- General construction process
- Builder information
- Warranty information
- Financing information and pre-qualification
- Information on "Selling Your Current Home"
- Details about the Sales Executive

Although you set the expectations up front, many interested buyers will call or e-mail you and ask when you expect the neighborhood to open and the prices of the homes. Usually, the actual opening date is an estimate up until a few weeks before it actually happens. Also, prices are not usually determined until the opening date is set because of fluctuations.

Here are some scripts you can use to answer these questions to the customer's satisfaction and still keep them interested.

Regarding Grand Opening

"Thank you for your interest in _____ community. We are expecting the Grand Opening some time in _____. However, at this time, we do not have an exact date because we are still finalizing the community details and floor plans.

I would like to keep you informed by sending you the latest updates on _____ community. As soon as I know more details, I will send you that information via e-mail. How does that sound?

Regarding Home Prices

"At this time, we do not have the investment range set for _____ community. We are expecting this community to start in the low $250,000's, but since we do not know the opening date, we cannot set those prices quite yet.

I would like to keep you informed by sending you the latest updates on _____ community. As soon as we have our pricing set, I will be sure to send you an e-mail. How does that sound?

It is also important to call customers to verify their interest when they first register for your Priority List. During this call, confirm that they are actually interested in this new neighborhood or help them find a community that better meets their needs. You will often find that customers think this might work, but keep waiting, only to find out this new community is not the right style, price, or size. Once you have additional information, you might find another community will be a better fit.

CHAPTER SUMMARY

The goal of any Online Sales Program is to gain permission from your customers and turn them into buyers. A pre-sale campaign is an effective way to capture those browsers and increase sales momentum even before a community has a model home. Timing is critical. Start the buzz early and watch your Priority List grow. Market to them effectively and persistently and you will be pleased with the results.

Chapter Thirteen

MEASURING
SUCCESS

Tracking and reporting of the online sales program

One of the key benefits of an Online Sales Program is the ability to track and quantify actual results. Because you can measure results in every area, it is imperative that you spend time understanding the statistics so you can test and change the program to produce better results.

The three key metrics to measure and track results are:

- **Online Sales Counselor:** appointments and contracts
- **Website Statistics:** site usage and conversion rates
- **Online Marketing Statistics:** effectiveness of marketing sources

Many of these statistics will be used in conjunction with each other.

Appointments and Contracts

This is one area that should be easy to track. Your OSC is paid from the result of these measurements so s/he should be able to stay on top of it. The key areas to track are:

- Appointments set
- Appointments kept
- Appointments missed
- Contracts from appointments
- Closings from appointments

- Ratio of online contract to onsite contracts
- Ratio of online closings to onsite closings
- Leads who visited but did not schedule with OSC
- Percentage of leads from website's unique visitors

These metrics will help you to evaluate the effectiveness of both your OSC and your Online Sales Program.

The OSC will track the initial appointment set and will need a confirmation from the onsite agent after the appointment is held to verify that the prospect visited the community. If the lead management software you choose does not allow the onsite agent to update the status of the appointment, the OSC can send a quick e-mail after the appointment time, verifying that the prospect made it to the appointment. This is also a good time to make sure the prospect liked the neighborhood and does not need further information. A well-trained OSC will follow up with the lead if the appointment was missed or they did not like the neighborhood and will try to set another appointment.

By comparing and tracking the percentages of sales driven from your Online Sales Program, you will be able to justify the amount of marketing dollars spent to acquire these customers.

I recommend creating two reports: one for the appointments set (to be used for commission tracking) and another for the conversion ratios for the leads. If your CRM does not have this capability, use a multi-page report created in Excel that combines data from each report in the different areas.

Website Statistics

Measuring the effectiveness of your website will give you a clear picture of how your customers are using the site and what they are using the most.

You will also be able to track conversion rates and actions to see how those customers made their decisions.

Here are some of the key metrics you should be observing and tracking on your site:

- **Unique Visitors:** The total number of individuals to your site (not to be confused with "Hits", which includes repeat views from the same people)
- **Return versus New Visitors:** The number of actual new customers you acquire versus the visitors who have already been to your site
- **Conversions:** The number of total visitors who have a conversion action and where the lead was generated
- **Conversion Funnel:** The sequence of pages that encouraged a conversion action
- **Length of Visit:** The length of time each visitor stays on your site (also called "stickiness")
- **Number of Pages Viewed:** The number of pages each visitor views per visit
- **Top Pages:** The pages most often viewed by visitors
- **Entry and Exit Pages:** The pages on which the visitors enter and exit the site; this can reveal interesting patterns in your site
- **Search Engine Traffic:** The specific organic search and PPC results that are the most popular
- **Referrers:** Those websites that refer customers to your website

You will need website analytics software to track and view these statistics.

Google Analytics is one of the most common tools used and is a free option.

Now that you have the ability to track and view results, you can begin testing different scenarios on your site and measure the effectiveness of each. Change the message on your front page to see what drives greater results. Adjust the calls to action to determine what gets the customer's attention. Focus on what drives the most conversions and diligently review your statistics.

Most analytics software will allow you to set up conversion or goal tracking. A conversion occurs when a visitor completes an activity that you have identified as important, such as e-mail list registration, a download, or viewing an online presentation. This can usually be measured by having your website developer install a tracking code on pages like the "Contact Thank You Page" or "User Registration Page".

Once you have the conversion goals set up, start tracking what drives people to these goals and the sources that produce the highest conversion numbers.

This leads us into the final area of tracking.

Online Marketing Statistics

The ability to specifically track and measure success of marketing sources is one of the most valuable benefits of online advertising and marketing. You can determine the return on investment simply by measuring the amount of traffic a source drives to your website and the conversion rate from that traffic. Let's take a look at how this can be used.

Marketing Source	Cost	Traffic	Conversion Rate	Total Leads
Banner Ad	$ 1000	1000	1%	10
PPC	$ 500	600	3%	18
Online Classified	$ 0	400	2%	8

As you can see in this over simplified example, the largest ROI comes from the Online Classified Listing because it is free and produced eight leads. This information really comes in handy when comparing one paid online marketing source with another. There is no reason to spend money in areas that deliver low results.

Tracking PPC Results

If you are managing your search engine marketing internally, you will need to continually track and change your pay-per-click search engine marketing. All PPC avenues like Google, Yahoo, and Bing have highly detailed tracking that allows you to determine the best ROI. Anyone can throw up a PPC campaign, pay a lot of money, and receive more website traffic. However, the true measure of success is the conversion rate of that traffic. For example, you could bid on many real estate keywords that would produce more traffic. However, these prospects may only be in the market for a used home or a home that is ready now. So, the conversion rates might be substantially lower than those from other marketing sources. That's not to say you shouldn't purchase real estate keywords. You will just need to be strategic by monitoring the bid price and keeping the PPC ad descriptive.

To effectively track the results, make certain that you have the conversion or goal tracking set up to track which keywords produce the highest conversion rate.

Tracking Marketing Results

With your Online Sales Program in place, you should allocate a fair amount of your marketing budget to online sources. One area that is imperative to track are the third-party referral sites. A key benefit of these sites is the ability to track and connect the lead source with a customer, along with the corresponding appointments and contracts that result from these leads.

This is accomplished because users are required to enter their information at the referral site in order to ask questions or request information on the homes or communities. With this information, you can measure the effectiveness of these sources and adjust the budget allocation to make sure your investment is placed where it earns the best return.

Shopping Your Own Website

When you are looking to increase your conversions, think like a customer, and personally shop your own and your competitors' websites.

You're marketing online—and maybe even taking advantage of an Online Sales Counselor to increase prospect interaction, response, and conversions. You're probably starting to realize it's no longer okay to just sit back and wait for homebuyers to come a-knocking. Today's online marketing options evolve and improve almost hourly, so if you want to make sure you're focusing your online marketing efforts in the right areas, it's critical to keep up with what your competitors are doing.

The alternative? Being left behind in a huge cloud of technology dust. Here are a few quick tips that every manager/OSC should be doing on a regular basis.

Google (yes it's a verb) new homes in your area to see how you stack up.

In a few seconds, you can do a Google search for "new homes [your town]" and see how you rank in the search results (or if you rank at all). You'll get a glimpse of your competitors' offerings and maybe even discover some new options for listing properties in other areas.

Just keep in mind that results and rankings change regularly, so make sure you constantly optimize your site for easy access by Google and other top search engines. Don't forget Yahoo!, Bing, and others.

Don't trust third-party sources for accurate, up-to-date listings.

Do you list your homes on third-party sites like Newhomesource.com? Search these sites for homes in your area as if you're a customer to make sure your listings are current and accurate. Try searches in different areas and investment ranges. These websites don't have time to keep up with everyone's inventory, so make sure you check back with them often to make sure your listings are up to date and correct.

Try to "break" your website with a critical test-drive.

Curious how your site performs when a potential customer is searching for a home? Again, put yourself in their shoes—or at least in their web browser. Fire up your site with a critical eye, as if you're seeing it for the first time. Then, ask yourself:

- Is the navigation intuitive?
- Are communities and floorplans easily accessible?
- Are any of the links "dead"?
- Are any of the pages—or listed properties—outdated?

Nothing is more frustrating to a prospect than an outdated website. One of your most important online marketing jobs is to MONITOR AND UPDATE EVERYTHING constantly. At the same time, make sure your company's important features and promotions are properly highlighted—and that navigation is part of the solution (instead of a sales-blocker).

Keep track of competitors, too.

It's easy to become complacent and think that the online homebuilder marketing universe revolves around you. It's human nature, but it's also one of the great barriers to expanding your horizons—and your success. Keeping an eye on your competitors' sites is one of the best ways to learn about new features, programs, and marketing strategies you may be able to leverage for your business.

Submit a request—of your OWN company. Okay, so you send out hundreds of e-mails a month. But are you on the receiving end of your own marketing campaigns? You should be. Just remember: "Out of sight, out of mind." Include your own contact information in all your marketing campaigns—automated or otherwise—to make sure your messaging is concise, properly targeted, and correctly delivered. In your new "consumer" mindset, you may realize you don't like the tone, phrasing, or even the overall content of the communications you're sending out to represent your company.

Conduct periodic reviews of the online marketing landscape.

Over time, for various reasons, web-based programs and processes for marketing your business online will break down and stop working. By far, the best way to check your entire web marketing ecosystem is to regularly conduct new home searches via your own site—as well as those of your top competitors. Just make sure that SOMEONE in your organization is the "point person" for periodic reviews of the online marketing landscape.

Remember, today's web-savvy customers are already comparing you to your online competitors, so you might as well see what they're seeing. In this way, you can proactively plan new programs and quickly react to competitive developments.

Secret Shop Your Online Sales Program

When I ask sales managers or owners if they have shopped their sales people, most will say "yes". I am not talking about a physical shop at a model home, but an online shop. When I clarify this point, many say, **"Well no, we have never done that. Should we?"** In which case, I kindly respond, **"Heck. YES!!!"**

Surveys show us that about half of sales executives don't follow up with an online lead and roughly three out of four will never pick up a phone to call. So, it is crucial that you periodically shop your sales executives to get an idea of what is happening online and over the phone. This is especially true for the Online Sales Counselor. Here is a quick tutorial on how to set up a virtual shop:

- Set up a secret shopper Gmail account.
- Get a Google Voice number and attach it to your new Gmail account.
- Go to your web form during business hours and submit your secret shopper's information along with a question.
- Sit back and tally the results.

Once you've set up a secret shopper account through Gmail, test it by sending an e-mail and making a phone call before you submit your online shop. Make sure you've gone into settings so that Google Voice is set on "Do Not Disturb"; messages will then be recorded, transcribed, and sent to your inbox. All call attempts will be sent there as well.

After testing your e-mail and phone number, you are ready to submit your secret shop during business hours to give your sales agents a fair shot at answering quickly and efficiently.

During the shop, look for key qualifiers that will allow you to gauge the effectiveness of the follow up program:

- **Speed of response:** A personal response should come within the first hour of sending the inquiry; however a response in five minutes or less is 100 times more likely to turn the inquiry into a responsive lead.
- **Quality of communication:** Are the e-mails and phone calls you receive engaging, friendly, and helpful?
- **Frequency of response:** The first week is critical; overall in the first month, you should track seven points of contact. 80 percent of sales

are made between the fifth and the twelfth contact, yet fewer than 10 percent of sales executives will ever make more than three contacts to a prospect before they give up.

The Phone Shop

After a month of follow-up via e-mail and phone, you should then phone shop your agents to see how they go about trying to set an appointment over the phone. You can do this through a number of methods, but the easiest way to record a phone call is with a Skype account. There are lots of Skype recording options out there, including the MX SkypeRecorder (which is free), PowerGramo, or Ecamm.

In evaluating the shop, look for first e-mails and phone calls that are returned promptly after your inquiry. After that, you want persistent and consistent follow-up. If this is not what you are seeing, then some online and phone sales training may be in order to get the results you want.

Ask yourself this question when reviewing the shop results: "How is my company represented?" If you aren't satisfied, make a change!

CHAPTER SUMMARY

No marketing campaign is successful unless you can measure the results. Online marketing allows campaigns to be created, tracked, and changed quickly and efficiently. As you invest more, you will need to measure and adjust more. With the technology changing so quickly, it is a necessity to stay on top of your numbers.

CALL
TO ACTION

"Ideas are worthless unless you act upon them."

—Earl Nightingale

You have just been given the secrets to implementing a successful Online Sales Program. What will be your next step? Most of you have great intentions, but, as you know, intentions will not make this program successful. Only execution will produce the results you expect.

When you invest the time, energy, and resources to implement this program, you will see dramatic results. You also must include all of the ingredients of the Online Sales Formula to experience an increase in sales.

Countless times, I have heard the same story: "We invested all this money in a website and nothing is happening." Or "We have all these leads, but our onsite sales agents can't set appointments."

Take a hard look at your current program and fill in the gaps. Once you incorporate all of the components and have a dedicated person managing these browsers, your ratios will improve.

This is only taking into consideration the current market of buyers. Next year's buyer will use the Internet more and expect more. This reflects a shift in the world of real estate. Buyers today expect more information and better service.

Not only will this program increase your sales, but the program itself will also expand over time. One person will not be able to handle all of the leads and you will need to grow this position into a department.

So, do not waste time. Educate yourself. Stay ahead of the curve. Be an innovator. This idea is not new, but taking action in this area may be new to you. However, it's necessary if you want to set yourself apart from your competition!

BEST OF THE
BLOG

Over the years I have written articles but they didn't fit neatly into the previous chapters. So I guess I will just shove them in here at the end. Take a look at these blog posts from www.doyouconvert.com that might give you even more insight into succeeding in this online universe.

The Quest for Inbox Zero

Does your inbox make your sales efforts inefficient? Increased response time— is the best way to keep your potential conversions from competitors.

Every Sales Consultant recognizes the critical value of customer response times. They're absolutely key to converting leads before your competition can. This is especially true in today's ultra-competitive "e-mail-text-IM-it-now" business environment where prospects and customers expect almost instant responses.

That's why one of any Sales Consultant's worst enemies is a cluttered, disorganized e-mail inbox. I know (from experience) that it's not the easiest thing in the world to stay organized—and ready to pounce on hot leads—if you can't even tell which message is your top priority. And with all your daily tasks, reminders, and appointments chiming away, how can you possibly keep it all clear on screen and in your mind?

Remember, a lead is always a good thing,
no matter how busy you are.

When the volume of e-mail messages becomes overwhelming and your "to do" list seems to be spinning out of control, you'll actually end up experiencing a *negative* emotional response each time you receive a new lead. Imagine that—instead of being excited at a new opportunity, you slump in your chair and mumble, "Here comes another lead; great—*just one more thing to add to my list."*

I recently re-read a modern classic—David Allen's book *"Getting Things Done".* In this book, David offers a fantastic new system for managing your time and increasing your productivity. He also serves up a great system for taming the ole' inbox using the same techniques.

To give you a taste of David's insights, here is a brief overview on how you can take advantage of his innovative principles to change your e-mail habits, so you'll be perfectly prepared to calmly handle every new message that comes your way.

Experience the business-boosting freedom of an uncluttered inbox.

Simply put, I can't tell you how freeing it is to have an empty inbox. The concept is to get rid of those "sticky" e-mails—you know, the ones that you can't do anything about, aren't quite ready to handle, and really just distract you from responding to higher priority tasks. David's rules basically boil down to three simple steps—see a new e-mail, read it, and immediately decide what to do with it.

Here are five choices for dealing with a message the moment it lands in your inbox:

- **Delete it.** Seriously, this will probably cover most of your e-mails. Immediately toss out all those forwards, CC's , Facebook updates, Twitter follows, and messages that don't even interest you. Become an e-mail Zen master, at one with your "Delete" key. Free up that inbox for messages that will potentially make you the most money—not time-wasters like the latest Justin Bieber video.

- **Answer it.** If you can respond effectively in two minutes or less to a message requiring a follow-up, take care of it right then and there. It doesn't matter if it's a reply to a customer, an associate, or even a personal e-mail. Just make sure it doesn't take you more than a minute or two.

- **Defer it.** You'd be amazed at how many of the e-mails sent your way aren't even your responsibility. Ask yourself, "Am I really the right person for this job?" If not, figure out who is, and pass the message on. You might also respond to the sender and copy in the responsible party, just to make sure everyone is on the same page. Of course, make sure that the responsible party is actually accepting responsibility— especially if you are delegating a task.

- **Save it.** Some e-mails won't need action—but they don't deserve the instant "Delete" treatment either—like passwords, e-mail newsletters, and receipts. You might need these messages in the future, so create a folder or folders to store these for future reference. The great thing about all the latest e-mail programs is that you can perform searches to find those old e-mails anytime you want.

- **Determine the next action.** If a message requires action, but a response will take longer than two minutes, move it to an "Action" folder. Then, create a new task for the action item related to the next step for that message. This way, you get to keep a message AND get "permission" to forget about it until the task is at hand—later that day, that week, or that month. It sure beats the heck out of opening up your inbox every day and wasting valuable time and brainpower staring at a wall of e-mails asking, "What do I need to do with all these again?"

E-mail is the primary lifeline to prospects and buyers. That's why it so important to keep our "virtual" desk clutter-free—organization leads directly to higher productivity. Naturally, your inbox will fill up while you are away from your desk. Just make sure that you zip through it and trim down your incoming emails at least twice a day, so you're back at square one and ready for the next lead, question, or response.

This simple technique has eliminated LOADS of stress emanating from my bulging, unorganized e-mail inbox. Before, it seemed like every time I opened my account, I didn't know where to start.

I highly recommend reading David Allen's book, *"Getting Things Done: The Art of Stress-Free Productivity"*, and purchasing the companion manual (GTD and Outlook) to help you restructure your inbox—and seriously streamline your prospect response times for increased sales.

How To Generate Your Own Leads

Those of you who have been in the business of selling for a while realize that the job description and requirements have changed dramatically.

Back in the day, if you could conduct a decent presentation and ask some closing questions, you could make a comfortable income. Way, way back in the day, you didn't even need that much; you just needed to be pleasant and write a contract.

The business of selling homes nowadays has shifted significantly. Just as the responsibilities have changed for builders and brokers, salespeople now have to do a lot more with a lot less.

It used to be, if you were a new home sales agent, you would show up on site, open the doors, turn on all the lights, and wait for the traffic to walk through the door. Thanks to the endless marketing dollars flowing out of the builders' pockets, it was a safe bet that you'd sell a few houses each month. But now, the marketing budgets are dwindling and sales agents have to be more resourceful if they are going to keep their numbers up and, in some cases, keep their jobs.

One of the key differentiators for a sales executive and the easiest way to make yourself indispensable is if you **have a plan for your own lead generation**. What I mean by lead generation is this: **the ability to self-generate your own prospects without relying on an outside marketing plan or dollars.**

This is not a new concept, but one that I believe has become vital to the success of any sales person.

Here are three simple steps to create your own lead generation plan.

Step One: Become the recognized expert.
What could you be the expert on? You might be the one who knows new construction inside and out. You might be the "green building" expert. Or maybe you're the expert on your community and area. As you establish yourself as an expert, you will see heightened awareness. In order to do this, you need to publish great articles on your own blog, be active and connected on social networking sites, create a monthly e-mail newsletter for all of your new connections, and take your networking offline as well. Build your reputation as the one to call for _____ (fill in the blank with your area of expertise). With this new awareness will come referrals and phone calls.

Step Two: Generate referrals by being remarkable.
Often overlooked but critical to success, focusing on the referrals from past customers is a key task. Now, referrals are a tricky one. Everybody talks about referrals, but many sales executives drop the ball between the time they sell a home and when they need to ask for a referral. **It's pretty awkward to ask for a referral when there's been no memorable communication after the close.**

So how can you be remarkable enough to earn a referral? Communication is key. Memorable communication leads to great customer service, which in turn, leads to the right to ask for a referral. Are you responsive? Did you shoot videos of the home for the customer? Did you send pictures to your prospects? Did you call enough?

The great thing about technology is that it allows us to be creative and think outside the box to appeal to our prospects and create a strong first, second, and third impressions.

We often just forget to communicate with our past customers because we are focused on current prospects. Utilize your systems to stay in touch with your past customers and watch your referrals go through the roof. My favorite way to ask for the referral, "Do you have any friends who might want to live next to you?"

Step three: Have a follow-up plan for self generated leads.
You come back from the networking event with a handful of real estate agents' cards. People are referring their friends to you. You have all these newfound opportunities, but no specific process to stay in touch. Some will buy, some won't. Unless you have a crystal ball to see who will be your buyers, you have to stay in touch.

Creating agent relationships doesn't happen overnight. If you don't put a process in place to communicate with each lead over the next month, the lead that you generated is worthless. A prospect's buying cycle may be long; if you don't have a specific plan for short and long-term follow up, you will miss a sale.

If you walk in the door to any interview and show them a specific plan for lead generation, you will place yourself in the top one percent of sales executives out there. If you execute that plan you will earn yourself a successful career!

Execution of a plan is always the hard part. Spending time on this every day is what it takes to be successful. Be diligent, be memorable, and be active, and you'll see your awareness increase along with your sales.

Don't curb-qualify your leads.

A little bit of information can be dangerous—like when sales people do a quick scan of someone who walks in the door and immediately calculate that individual's ability and desire to buy. By curb-qualifying leads, they make snap judgments based on very little knowledge.

Question: Have you ever been proven wrong? Be honest!

You might also curb-qualify someone who calls you for more information about your homes. Maybe you're really that good at evaluating prospective buyers. But are you willing to bet a sale that you're batting .1000 in this ballpark?

Do you give first-rate attention to third-party leads?

Let's say you're getting information requests from third-party sources or listing sites. You might be supplied limited data, possibly just an e-mail address. A lot of sales professionals I know will say, "Man, those third-party sites never produce good leads. Those prospects never call me back. They never respond at all."

That's because we haven't taken the all-important step of understanding why these consumers are submitting information requests at this particular time. It's your job to nurture a lead and cultivate the relationship while they continue their search and close in on the purchase of a new home.

They are calling because they need more information in order to make decisions. They might not be as enthusiastic as you'd like, or ready to jump into the buying process, but that doesn't mean this new home sales prospect is a dead end. The last thing you should do in this case is to prejudge based on a brief phone conversation. Don't shrug them off with, "Eh, nothing's going to happen with this one."

I see it all the time. There's a disconnect when it comes to setting clear expectations of what these sales prospects can and will produce. Only 20 to 25 percent of them will ever come in to an on-site appointment. Just because many of them fizzle, don't assume there are no sweet leads in this group. To get results, you need a system in place to follow up in a consistent and persistent manner.

My best advice to you is to think carefully about how you view these online leads. Reframe your mindset, if necessary, so that you don't ever curb-qualify your online leads again. When you make this change, you'll see an increase in appointments and in sales.

Create New Prospects with Effective Call and E-mail Campaigns

Are you looking for affordable ways to drum up new business? Many marketing and sales departments are huddled in their conference rooms, brainstorming ways to generate new business.

In most housing markets, you still have a good percentage of shoppers out there looking for their next home. So how do you guide them to you? One logical solution would be to launch an e-mail campaign or phone call "blitz" to connect with past prospects and shift them into higher gear.

The question is, are you getting the right results from your efforts? Too often, these campaigns are poorly executed with the wrong strategy, weak message, no call to action, or no connection with the front line sales team. With this reality in mind, here are a few ideas to help you drive better responses from your e-mail and call campaigns.

Think "Prospecting"

The new age of selling requires everyone to generate their own leads. Don't rely solely on your marketing department for the message. Take the time to craft your own marketing messages to use via e-mail and phone. Create your e-mail templates; it's easy with e-mail service providers like MailChimp, Constant Contact, and iContact. Be sure to include a powerful subject line and open with a catchy intro to grab their attention. Keep it personal but remember, time is a precious commodity—for both you and your prospect—so prepare in advance. Don't get on a call without a practiced phone script and a voice-mail message ready to go.

Build Momentum By Starting with the Right People.

Approach your more likely prospects first. Build a quality list of interested people who want to hear from you and start with them.

Focus on decision-makers. If a prospect tells you they need to speak with a spouse/significant other, ask if there might be a good time to talk with them on the phone. This is a common objection, so dig deeper to see if they have other reasons for pushing back.

Have a Good Reason to Connect.

Before you click or dial, have a clear, powerful reason for initiating this contact. Be very specific in your message to prospects when you connect. The desired next step is to generate the in-person appointment. Don't just call to chat during a call campaign. That will only slow you down.

Practice Smart Time Management.

Set aside non-interrupted time to focus on your goal of calling and e-mailing. Make this time productive by avoiding distractions. These campaigns require a weekly time allotment if you want results. Don't just leave this important business development task to be squeezed in when it is "convenient" because you'll just push it aside.

Prepare a Follow-up Strategy.

Follow-up is essential and expected. So what happens when you prompt a response from a prospect? Be prepared to react by having your follow-up strategy in place. You will stay on track when you have your responses and next steps ready beforehand. Momentum is important. Don't compromise it with lack of preparedness.

Keep up the frequency. Most sales agents fade away after one to three contacts. Remember, it will take five to seven touches to generate a response, so keep the communication going.

Call and then e-mail—e-mail and then call. The two should always be connected. After you send the e-mail, pick up the phone and call the customer to let them know you are trying to reach them.

Are you going to take advantage of the opportunity to catapult your call and e-mail campaigns into successful lead generating campaigns? Put your plan in place and then make it happen!

Home Buying Process From A Woman's Perspective

It is no secret that, in most families, when it comes to decision-making—or for a better term, money spending—the woman "wears the pants". If you are a homebuilder or real estate agent trying to sell these homes, you need to know the deal breakers in this process. So here is a glimpse inside the female mind when it comes to finding a real estate agent and a home, from the smartest woman I know, my wife ,Cori:

"My loving husband asked me to write this blog. He wanted a blog about my home buying process and experience. I say 'my experience', because I am the one who does the leg work, decides where we want to be, looks at the homes, narrows it down, and then I have Mike come for final approval to make him feel like he has a say in things.

Schools Rule

The first thing I do when home shopping is to decide which school we want to be close to. I use GreatSchools.net to research schools in the area and to find the exact school I want my kids to go to. After narrowing down the schools, the home shopping starts.

Unfortunately, there aren't websites out there where you can search for a home by a specific school (school district, yes, but not specific school). In order to narrow your search to a school, you have to use a realtor. I get the zip code for the school I want and go to Realtor.com and I conduct my search there. I also tap into my social media resources—going on Facebook and say, 'Anyone buy a home in _____ district? What about _____ school district?'

Give Me the Details…Like Now!

If I'm looking for a new home, I will search online for homebuilders, check out their websites—focusing on floor plans, price ranges, and locations. My husband teases that marketing was created for people like me. I choose services and products based on the website. I have two kids and not much time. If the site is confusing, I won't stick with it to figure it out. If the information I need isn't on the site, the chances of me calling to find out the basics are slim to none.

'Do You Know Who I Am?' Be Professional and Follow Up

Once the list is narrowed down based on the information I find online, I will call for specifics or make an appointment. Again, I have two kids. If I don't get a response in the following 24 hours, I will probably forget I ever called and I will mark you off my list. If I make time to contact you, it means I am ready to buy and I will not wait around for a response. E-mail is wonderful—I can get information while juggling kids, but phone calls are also great.

I once looked at over five homes by calling each listing agent and scheduling an appointment. Not one person was on time, let alone early enough to prepare the home for a walk through. If I am able to be there on time with my kids in tow, I expect the same courtesy. When I got to the sixth home, it was open and ready, and the agent handed me info on herself and the home. She was able to answer all my questions and right there on the spot, she became my agent. Everyone is busy—timeliness is vital.

Another thing that drives me bananas are agents and salespeople who don't know the answers to my questions or do not get the information to me in a timely manner. Know the basics and, if I ask an obscure question, no biggie, but get me the info and soon!

Most importantly, follow up! It really does work. If I contact you, I want to hear from you. AND I will remember you. I will go about my day, think of a question to ask you, forget that question and then I get an e-mail from you and BAM, I remember.

The Internet was invented for women like me. I can get more done with my kids. If you are in the places where I am, I will see you. If you have a good website, good follow-up and helpful sales people, I will love you!

Bonus:

BEST PRACTICES
FOR ACHIEVING FIRST-PAGE SEARCH RESULTS

By Jim Adams

Most real estate professionals know by now that 90 percent of home buyers are conducting their research online before they go out to physically visit a home (National Association of Realtors). But with billions of pages on the internet and millions of pages added each day, how do we get those consumers to find your website? The internet has become completely intertwined into the American culture and using search engines has become our number one Internet activity (Pew Research).

Consider the following:
- 76 percent of Americans are online (InternetWorldStats.com)
- 15.5 billion searches are performed each month (comScore). That's 660 million searches each hour and 11 million searches each minute

With all that searching, 96 percent of consumers never make it past the first page of search results (iCrossing). That first SERP (search engine results page) has become the beachfront property of the internet. The first page is where the influence happens and where the money is made. If your homes are found on the first page of an internet search, you have a distinct advantage over competitors who are not found. Internet search is uniquely critical in modern real estate, for one overarching reason: No one is just driving around looking for homes anymore. Instead, buyers do their research online first. Then, after filtering out the homes that don't meet their criteria, they pay the property a visit. The bottom line: If you're not found on the web, you don't exist.

Search Engine Optimization (SEO) is critical

Consumers have made it clear that it's critical to be found in the natural (non-paid) search results. Consider the following statistics:

- 86 percent of all Google clicks come in the form of non-paid, organic listing clicks (Avinash Kaushik).
- 85 percent of company budgets are spent on paid, sponsored listings (Forrester Research).
- Google users have indicated they prefer organic listings over paid listings at the rate of 70 percent to 30 percent.

You can see the vast discrepancy between where consumers are clicking and where companies are spending their money. Companies need to spend more money on SEO to take advantage of this gigantic opportunity.

SEO types

There are two types of SEO: on-site optimization and off-site optimization—also referred to as internal optimization and external optimization, or on-page and off-page optimization, respectively. On-site optimization has to do with site components such as title tags, description tags, and the content of your website—things you can control. Off-site optimization deals with other websites that link to yours; you rarely have control over this. Both are of equal importance in the complete SEO picture.

Keyword research

Keyword research is the foundation for all natural search engine optimization techniques. The objective is to know what search terms are reaching your target audience. A chosen list of keywords will ultimately be selected based on search volume and ability to compete for those terms. Don't start optimizing until you know for sure what keywords you need.

I caution you against taking this lightly. It does no good to optimize for something no one is looking for.

When researching keywords, you should:

Think like consumers

What would a normal person type in the search box to find your product? Consumers may use several variations, but it most likely will include the location (this is called geo-targeting) alongside terms such as "homes," "condos," "homes for sale," "real estate," "condos for sale," "foreclosures" or "new homes."

Other ways to think like your consumers:

- Brainstorm and list every phrase that might be used to find what your site offers.
- Ask friends and colleagues for suggestions.
- Poll your consumer base and get their input.

After hearing from these consumers, you may be surprised at the keywords they recommend. If that happens, resist the temptation to discard their input because chances are, the people you interviewed are the profile of your ideal customer. While the keywords they suggest may sound strange to you, bear in mind that most people use natural language in their searches. They don't use the industry terminology you and I know. They just want to find a home.

Validate with a keyword research tool

Use keyword research tools to confirm or deny your keyword list. Don't move on without doing this. Many times, business people think they know the best keywords. Business people also are more familiar with the industry terminology that consumers don't know or use. Confirm your instincts with a keyword research tool before progressing to the next step.

Here are keyword research tools you can use:

- Wordtracker Free Keywords (http://freekeywords.wordtracker.com/) provides free keyword suggestions from Wordtracker.
- Wordtracker (http://www.wordtracker.com/) also has a more advanced paid version, and sells top keyword reports.
- Google AdWords Keyword Suggestion Tool (https://adwords.google.com/ select/KeywordToolExternal) recommends keywords based on a keyword you enter or a URL you have the tool analyze.
- WordStream Keyword Tool (http://www.wordstream.com/keywords/) allows you to export a list of thousands of keywords for free.
- Keyword Discovery (http://www.keyworddiscovery.com/search.html) is a free keyword tool from Trellian.
- Trellian (http://www.keyworddiscovery.com/) also has a more advanced paid version of Keyword Discovery.
- Yahoo! Research Tool (http://advertising.yahoo.com/smallbusiness/ysm)
- YouTube Research Tool (https://ads.youtube.com/keyword_tool)

SEO essentials

Google calculates more than 100 components in its algorithm, but the most important components are:

- Title tag
- Description tag
- Content
- Inbound links

Consequently, these components should include your keywords if that page is to have pinpoint relevance. Most sites only include the keywords they're after in just one or two of the above components. A page with the targeted keywords in all four components will be considered more relevant than a page with the targeted keywords in only one of the above components. Get them all working together to create the strongest relevancy possible.

Title tags

A page's title tag tells consumers and search engines the topic of a particular page. If each web page is different, then each web page should have a unique title tag. Imagine each web page is a book, and Google is a library. Now imagine walking into that library, only to find books with no book titles. You might be able to navigate your way if you knew the author's name, but if you didn't have that handy, finding information would be extremely difficult.

Book titles tell us what the book is about. Web page titles tell search engines what the page is about. **The title tage is the most important element a search engine uses to decide where a web page should be displayed in the search results.** When an accurate title is present, it's much easier to figure out what this book is about.

The title tag is placed between the <head></head> tags of the web page.

```
<html>
```

```
<head>
```

```
<title> (Your City) New Homes & (Your City) Homes For Sale –
(Company name) </title>
```

```
</head>
```

```
<body>
```

TIP: Each web page should have a unique title, even if it's only slightly different. Within the entire website, no two title tags should be identical.

If your web page appears within a search results page, the title tag will appear on the first row of the results. Words searched by the user will be bolded in the web page's title. This assists users in recognizing relevant web pages.

Description tags

The page's description tag gives search engines a summary of the page's content. Like the title tag, the description tag is also an HTML meta tag, located within the <head> tag. <html>

```
<head>
```

```
<meta name=,"Description," content=," New Homes For Sale in
(your city). Search (your city) real estate, new homes, school
information and much more at (company name).>
```

```
</head>
```

```
<body>
```

This tag is often displayed on the search results page.

The description tag offers a lengthier summary of the title tag and, like the title tag, is also a contributing element to search engine results. Additionally, because description tags are displayed on search engine results pages, writing thoughtful and accurate description tags will have a strong impact on consumer click-through rates.

Site content

The content of your website will influence your site visitors—and search engines—more than anything else. As a rule, the search terms you are targeting need to appear in the content of the site, in the exact same order in which a search query is performed (not necessarily with every usage, but it should appear that way at least once). If the search term you are targeting is not on the page in the form of text, that page most likely will not displayed in the search engine results.

Inbound links

Many of us have heard of page rank, the original and distinct component Google uses in its algorithm. Page rank is also known as "Google Juice" and refers to the score that Google assigns to a particular web page; it is accumulated from inbound links from other websites. An inbound link is a link from a website other than your own that points to a page on your site. Inbound links are an important factor in how search engines determine how to rank sites.

There are two things to consider when building links to a site:

Linking sites should be of a similar theme. Sites linking to your site should be relevant to your site to maximize inbound link efforts. An inbound link that has little or nothing to do with your site will have much less positive impact—and could possibly have a negative one.

Links text should be relevant. Anchor text is the clickable text that is anchored to a hyperlink. Search engines look at the anchor text (keyword text) of a hyperlink to determine how to rank web pages. The more relevant the keyword within the hyperlink, the more valuable that link is. A common mistake is to use the text "click here" to define the actual link. It doesn't matter whether the links are internal or from other sites. Anchor text is very heavily weighted in a search engine's algorithm.

Maximizing the use of multiple sites

If you have two or more websites that share a common theme (i.e., real estate and mortgage), you can add to your sites' link portfolios by cross-linking between the sites. There are two methods of cross-linking. The first and most popular method is to place a link in the footer of all the primary site's pages. With this method, the same page on the secondary site will get all the links and the anchor text is the same for each link. If the primary site has 100 pages, and a link is placed in the footer from the primary site to the secondary site, the secondary site will have 100 links, all with the same anchor text.

The second method of cross-linking—and a far more effective way to build a site's link portfolio—is to cross-link in the content from individual pages on the primary site to a relevant page on the secondary site. Because anchor text is so heavily weighted in search engine algorithms, this linking method produces more effective results in search engine rankings. Wikipedia is an excellent example of how to cross-link from one page to another.

The concept is that you want to link from one page to another relevant page using anchor text that best describes the secondary page. This is effective for linking within your own site as well as secondary sites. In this way, you are most accurately describing your content to search engines, hence maximizing the available linking opportunities.

About Jim Adams

Jim Adams is the author of "The Little Black Book of SEO Secrets" and the founder and CEO of NewHomesDirectory.com. If you are smart, you'll pick up a copy of his book at http://www.jimadams.me/seobook/

SUMMARY

Search engine optimization presents a great opportunity for real estate companies to increase profitability by getting in front of the millions of people everyday who are searching for their next home. The greatest challenge to SEO is keeping up with the algorithmic changes of each search engine—these often happen daily. Google alone made between 350 and 550 changes in its organic search algorithms in 2009 (searchengineland.com). It takes time, money, and the right people to drive maximum profitability.

DO YOU CONVERT?

BROWSERS ▶ LEADS

LEADS ▶ APPOINTMENTS

APPOINTMENTS ▶ CONTRACTS

DO YOU CONVERT **BROWSERS TO BUYERS?**

FIND OUT HOW – Visit

www.DoYouConvert.com

ABOUT THE AUTHOR

Mike Lyon has "real world" knowledge and first-hand experience in the realm of online marketing and sales for homebuilders. He delivers his information from the trenches and draws from his diverse background in online advertising, digital design and internet sales.

With his energetic and entertaining speaking style, Mike has brought to life the topics of internet marketing, sales, and technology at events across the country and is one of the most requested speakers for online technology and tools for the home building industry.

Mike is a highly sought-after consultant and has contributed to the success of homebuilders and real estate companies all across the nation.

He is also the author of *Social Media Guide For Real Estate*.

Your comments, questions and ideas are welcome.

E-mail: solutions@doyouconvert.com

Website: www.DoYouConvert.com

LinkedIn: www.linkedin.com/in/mikelyon

Twitter: @mikelyon